A Quotation Collection

For our friends Jes and Jane with vivid memories of 'happy times'

Jim and Sally

June 2025

A Quotation Collection

Jim Dale

Acresfield Publishing

Published in January 2025 by Acresfield Publishing

Copyright © Jim Dale

The moral right of the author has been asserted. All rights reserved. Without limiting the right under copyright reserved above, no part of this publication may be reproduced, stored in or introduced into a retrieval system, or transmitted, in any form or by any means (electronic, mechanical, photocopying, recording or otherwise) without the prior written permission of both the copyright owner and the above publisher of this book.

Typeset by e-type

For my great friend Nick Cook

I have spent a couple of hours with Nick most Friday mornings for a good few years now, reading through this quotation collection page by page. Our process has been for me to read out a quotation, with Nick responding. He would draw out extensive literary and film insights, important historical references, wide-ranging personal connections born of a London life and a courageous Royal Navy career, entrepreneurial activity and the day's news. I responded and discussion ensued. Sometimes we would only get through a couple of pages or so before time was up. When we ultimately came to the end of the book, we would just start at the beginning again.

Crucially, Nick has enjoyed a lifetime of reading, largely history, biography and poetry. His ability to quote poetry is astonishing. But, above all, Nick is eminently sociable, with immense conversational skill, born of his life experiences, embracing a level of wit and humour which can break down barriers with anyone he meets, from any corner of our society, at any time. I am fortunate indeed to enjoy my Friday mornings with Nick, to whom I dedicate this book, as without his encouragement it would never have been published.

A memory of my Mother

It was my mother who gave me a beautiful leather-bound book for my birthday in May 1985, knowing I was going to put quotations into it. Across all the years since then, I filled it to the brim, predominantly drawing from the reading of books but also from newspapers, magazines, a Church bench and a plaque on the wall of her hospital room at the time of her death. So she played her part in the creation of this book, always supporting and encouraging my way ahead.

I thought I would celebrate her gift from all those years ago by using the quotation beneath to connect her description of the poverty she had seen as a child with a love of her own garden and the viewing of public gardens, which gave her immense pleasure in her later years. In my mind this is a message from her to me, which I now pass on to you.

If thou of fortune be bereft,
and in thy store there be but left
two loaves, sell one, and with the dole,
buy hyacinths to feed thy soul.

John Greenleaf Whittaker (1807-1892)

Author's Note

A quotation book really is like no other. From time to time throughout a life, we read children's books, school books, and we may read further education books, novels, biographies, poetry, history or whatever, but there is nothing which compares to a quotation book. Here you embark on a voyage of discovery, you delve into worlds other than your own to suit your mood or interests. You can cherry-pick your journey or you can read from beginning to end. The mind is a muscle and it has to be kept in trim. Here you have surprises at every turn of a page, lessons to be learned; ideas spring to mind, humour moves on to thoughtfulness and maybe sadness overcomes. I wish you well as you read these observations, taken from centuries gone by right through to our world today.

This quotation collection would never have been published without the professional assistance of Peter and Jayne Walsh of Milo Books, as well as considerable help from a number of others.

Gerry Radcliffe has lived with my collection for some years now, ultimately deciphering my handwriting as she typed up innumerable often over-filled pages of unintelligible scribble in order to progress it to publication. This was no mean feat and I owe her a very special debt of gratitude for doing it.

It was my daughter Emma who, with the benefit of artificial intelligence, fulfilled the necessary task of ensuring both accuracy and attribution. You would have had to have seen it for yourself to understand the level of chaotic congestion which prevailed on many of its pages. Undoubtedly her English Literature degree saved the day as she also introduced a much needed re-ordering across its pages. It was Melvyn Bragg who said, "English can carry you through a lifetime," and I am immensely grateful to her for devoting this knowledge to my quotation collection.

And throughout those years I have been surrounded by the love, interest and encouragement of my daughters Joanna and Sasha and my wife Sally. They have lived with it from beginning to end, supporting me all the way through with great patience and involvement when it was needed, recognising this collection represented the bringing together of my library, created from a lifetime's reading, with my mother's birthday present back in 1985. This, in its way, has been a gift of love from all my family and I can only thank them, from my heart, for it.

I have taken pains to corroborate facts and eliminate mistakes but, despite my best endeavours, I am aware there may still be errors. This is particularly the case regarding attribution. These quotations were collected across forty years, all put together before the thought of collating them into book form ever occurred to me. I am entirely and solely responsible for any errors or failures to fully clarify any information contained in this book.

Contents

Love, Relationships and Friendship	1
Freedom, Happiness and Virtue	14
Truth, Beauty and Art	26
Courage, Confidence and Gratitude	35
Faith, Fate and Hope	48
Success, Failure and Effort	66
Risk, Caution and Conformity	78
Time, Travel and Change	81
Education, Academia and Writing	89
Money, Business and Leadership	107
History, Politics and War	123
Evil, Anger and Despair	147
Life, Death and Suffering	151
Character, Experience and Words of Wisdom	164

Love, Relationships and Friendship

"The best portion of a good man's life
Is little, nameless unremembered acts of kindness and of love."
William Wordsworth

"Grief is the price we pay for love."
Queen Elizabeth II

"I am armed against love with a breastplate of reason."
Rufinus

"Love is not looking in each other's eyes but looking together in the same direction."
Antoine de Saint-Exupery

"Life is short: let us love one another: there is nothing else worth living for."
William Cory

"Human beings in love come nearer than in any of their other experiences to what we might conceive as absolutely good."
Noel Annan

"We have to take love where we find it, even if that means hours, days, weeks of disappointment and sadness. The moment we begin to seek love, love begins to seek us. And to save us."

Paulo Coelho

"Ah dear God, marriage is not a thing of nature, but a gift of God: the sweetest, the dearest, and the purest life above all celibacy and all singleness, when it turns out well, though the very devil if it does not!"

Martin Luther

"In marriage, being the right person is as important as finding the right person."

Wilbert D. Gough

"Divorce violates the present and desecrates the past. The energy of grief is awesome. I existed only for the children – that was my sense of it. But of course, children are never truly an 'only'; they are the best reason for existence, and being with them is the finest model we have to what it is to love. Every day, in large ways and small, they show us what it means."

Jennie Erdal

"They were equal because they were complementary."

Laurence Brander

"As I grew older, I found it easier to love people outside my family, and even people I do not know at all."

Denis Healey

LOVE, RELATIONSHIPS AND FRIENDSHIP

"There is no reciprocity. Men love women, women love children, children love hamsters."
Alice Thomas Ellis

"There is nothing nobler or more admirable than when two people who see eye to eye keep house as man and wife confounding their enemies and delighting their friends."
Homer

"She that is loved is safe and he that loves joyful."
Jeremy Taylor

"Our state cannot be severed; we are one,
One flesh; to lose thee were to lose myself."
John Milton

"You cannot legislate the heart; you can only contain it on sufferance for a while."
Unattributed

"The family is the most important unit in life."
Lord Denning

"The greatest thing a father can do for his children is to love their mother."
Josh McDowell

"The strongest binding love on the planet is a mother's love."
Andrew Marr

"Marriage is honourable in all."
Hebrews 13:4

"The first bond of society is marriage."
Cicero

"The 'usque ad finem' of marriage is a lifelong partnership that works."
Geoffrey Howe (*usque ad finem* meaning "to the very end")

"The advantage of being married to an archaeologist is that the older you get, the more interested he becomes in you."
Agatha Christie

"So, at the moment, and what a moment, I could look round at my children and grandchildren, whose ages range from 53 to 12. I could still trace my father's voice in their jokes, their laughter and their way with language. Their words will echo out into the future, with their children and their children's children. It's my father's claim to immortality – and mine also."
John Mortimer, reflecting on his daughter's wedding.

"It was the end of the New York city marathon and (a daughter) came toward the finish line. Another woman, older, stepped from the crowd … grasped the younger woman's hand and they held those clenched hands aloft running slowly towards the end. They were clearly mother and daughter … they ran as though someone had made a crack in the universe and mother and daughter were rushing toward it."
Louise Bernikow

"The result would be one of the most extraordinary partnerships in modern American political history. From the start the two men simply clicked. Kennedy liked Sorensen's cerebral approach; even more, he liked the pragmatic streak that ran through his liberalism. The young aide's definition of himself as someone moved less by sentimental than intellectual persuasion could have been the senator himself; ditto Sorensen's corollary assertion that 'the liberal who is rationally committed is more reliable than the liberal who is emotionally committed.' A tireless worker willing to put aside everything to advance Kennedy's career Sorensen became a kind of alter ego to the senator. He was the rarest of creatures: an aide who could work on the nitty-gritty of policy and also articulate the details in speeches and articles – the latter all under the senator's name alone – with simple fluency and grace. Soon it became hard to determine who had produced what, though one can think of them as the composer (Kennedy) and the lyricist (Sorensen). They were the Rodgers and Hart of politics. At twenty-four, and without the world exposure of his boss, Sorensen had neither the political experience nor the life experience to conceive the broad themes of speeches and articles – especially when they concerned foreign policy – but he was a quick student and a brilliant mimic, uncannily adept at finding just the historical allusion Kennedy wanted to express, the almost Churchillian cadences and spare language that embodied the senator's view of exemplary political rhetoric.

It wasn't mimicry alone, though. From the moment Sorensen arrived, Jack Kennedy's speeches took on a new flavour, combining a greater range of power and conclusion. They became more lyrical, more memorable, less burdened with data and detail. Long fascinated with the art of rhetoric and the secrets of superior orators, Kennedy would listen to recordings of Churchill and study the speeches of Lincoln, then talk with Sorensen about what he'd learned."

Fredrik Logevall on John F. Kennedy and Ted Sorensen

"Be kind. Remember everyone you meet is fighting a hard battle!"

Harry Thompson

"Only a few are able to live in delightful surroundings; the rest have to take things as they come. But will not the people of a continuing democracy awaken some time to the fact that they can possess as a community what they cannot as individuals."

Daniel Burnham

"I saved his life, and he behaved like an accountant."

Aristotle Onassis

"People love to be nice, but you must give them the chance."

Pierre-Auguste Renoir

"People let you down and, let's face it, you let others down – it's human nature."

Princess Alexandra, on the problems she faced with her daughter, Marina Ogilvy

"Never ask from where I came, nor what is my rank or name."

Daniel Schulman

"James is more cautious than I am, more of a statesman. He is Capricorn. If he were climbing a mountain, he'd follow the footpath. I would look for a short cut. I'm Taurus. We were both bachelors when we first met, and had a lot of fun together. He is a tremendous administrator, and brilliant at maintaining relationships between senior executives. The trust between us is enormous. If support is needed, it's there."

Gordon White on James Goldsmith

"'I think we did it for our mums,' I said. That's what he and I, with our very different backgrounds, had in common. We had both effectively lacked fathers in our households as we grew up. You try to succeed for those closest to you. When your grandparents struggled to escape adversity and persecution, when your parents put you on the right road and you have made something of your life, what remains? I think perhaps you need to use what you have to give meaning to their sacrifices by trying to make the world a better place for future generations – your own children and those of others."

Richard Desmond

"Many live wires would be dead ones if it were not for their connections."

The *Evening Standard*

"The word duty fell between us."

The Duke of Windsor

"I'm old fashioned enough to believe that you dance with the girl you came with."

Scott Turow

"Nothing can fill the gap when we are away from those we love, and it would be wrong to try and find anything. We must simply hold out and win through. That sounds very hard at first, but at the same time it is a great consolation, since leaving the gap unfilled preserves the bond between us. It is nonsense to say that God fills the gap: He does not fill it but keeps it empty so that our communion with another may be kept alive, even at the cost of pain."

Dietrich Bonhoeffer

"Americans and Britons are rather like in-laws, and what is really humiliating in this relationship – just when you get very grand and announce you will shake off the dust of their home for ever, is the maddening knowledge that they have a standing invitation for Christmas dinner."

Alistair Cooke

"In the end he felt as I did, that one lived one's life in isolation: one had to grapple with one's difficulties by oneself alone. I haven't that perfect gift of sympathy which he has, by which he knows intuitively what is going on in the other's mind. I wondered if I hadn't stifled something of this sensitiveness in myself, instead of perfecting it as he had done by his way of life and his belief in personal relations as the only reality."

Hugh Trevor-Roper on Isaiah Berlin

"Yet through it all, he only rarely allowed his will to falter; he focussed less on his own setbacks and suffering and more on how to end their root cause – the apartheid system of government – with an understanding that evolved over time that it could only happen if somehow he was able to develop meaningful relationships with those responsible for his treatment, both within the prison and, more importantly, within the political system."

Alaistair Campbell on Nelson Mandela

"You can have a serious life or a non-serious life, Teddy, I'll still love you whichever choice you make. But if you decide to have a non-serious life, I won't have much time for you. You make up your mind. There are too many children here who are doing things that are interesting for me to do much with you."

Joseph Kennedy

"If he is lucky in his chosen career, much of a man's life is his work. I have described that part of my life in my memoirs. Politics, however, is bound to bring frustration and disappointments which may ruin a man's happiness unless he can live in other worlds as well. I have been able to escape to nature and the arts, either of which could have been sufficient for me on their own if I had not chosen politics. But the main anchor of my equilibrium has been my love of my family. I have always preferred a private life to a social life, which is one reason I have often been regarded as a loner."

Denis Healey

"Make enemies; it's the cultural rule, because if you don't make enemies, you stand for nothing. And then eventually everyone's an enemy."

Andrew Marr

"More men die of jealousy than cancer."

Joseph P. Kennedy

"What count above all are personal relationships."
Siegmund Warburg

"Reconciliations are only possible when they are unnecessary."
Alexander Herzen

"Iron sharpens iron, and one man sharpens another."
Proverbs 27:17

"Father doesn't hear what Mother says and Mother hears what Father does not say."
John G. Murray

"Some people marry their opposites, others their mirror images. The latter damage themselves more, for in an incestuous marriage the virtues never seem to be strengthened as intensely as the vices."
Noel Annan

"A friend is needed when things are going badly. Anyone can be a friend of a successful man, who's done nothing wrong and is in the New Years Honours. But somebody who's in trouble, who's snapped and done something silly, that's when you need your friends."
John Aspinall

"Friendship with oneself is all important, because without it one cannot be friends with anyone else in the world!"
Eleanor Roosevelt

LOVE, RELATIONSHIPS AND FRIENDSHIP

"Every friend says, 'I too am your friend', but some are friends in name only. What a mortal grief it is when a dear friend turns into an enemy!"
Ecclesiasticus 37: 1-2

"What a pity that so many people are living with so few friends when the world is full of lonesome strangers who would give anything just to be somebody's friend."
Milo L. Arnold

"The sight of a friendly face in the great wilderness of London is a pleasant thing indeed to a lonely man."
Sir Arthur Conan Doyle

"Treat your friends as you do your pictures and place them in the best light."
Jenny Jerome Churchill

"It is chance that makes brothers, but hearts that make friends."
Emanuel von Geibel

"It is my belief that friendship is an experience too little explored."
Mary Warnock

"Human beings are born and die like animals or plants – but friends never die."
Siegmund Warburg

The relationship between very old friends is nearly always sad. They grow tired of and bored with each other."

James Lees-Milne

"It is not one's friends' virtues but their foibles which endear them to one."

Hugh Massingberd

"Women have a greater gift, I think, for friendship."

John Mortimer

"Do I not destroy my enemies when I make them my friends?"

Abraham Lincoln

"Yes, despite his aristocratic lineage, he was no snob. His closest friends came from a wide geographical and social background, including the son of a Canadian priest (Max Beaverbrook), a Welsh school teacher (Lloyd George), an Irish builder (Brendan Bracken), a Birkenhead estate agent (F. E. Smith), and an Alsatian engineer (Professor Lindemann)."

Andrew Roberts on Churchill

"Home, after all, is where your friends are."

Bruce Chatwin

"The sharpest moral lesson I learned was that, with very rare exceptions, loyalty between even the closest of friends vanished like a puff of smoke, when put under the slightest strain."

Charles Gordon

LOVE, RELATIONSHIPS AND FRIENDSHIP

"From quiet homes and first beginning,
Out to the undiscovered ends,
There's nothing worth the wear of winning,
But laughter and the love of friends."
Hilaire Belloc

"If I die tomorrow the thing I should be most grateful for in life would be my friendships."
Siegmund Warburg

Freedom, Happiness and Virtue

"Land of Hope and Glory
Mother of the free."

A.C. Benson

"Give me your tired, your poor, your huddled masses yearning to breathe free,
The wretched refuse of your teeming shore – Send these, the homeless, tempest-tost to me."

Emma Lazarus, inscribed on the Statue of Liberty

"In the future days, which we seek to make secure, we look forward to a world founded upon four essential human freedoms. The first is freedom of speech and expression—everywhere in the world. The second is freedom of every person to worship God in his own way—everywhere in the world. The third is freedom from want—which, translated into world terms, means economic understanding which will secure to every nation a healthy peacetime life for its inhabitants—everywhere in the world. The fourth is freedom from fear—which, translated into world terms, means a world-wide reduction of armaments to such a point and in such a thorough fashion that no nation will be in a position to commit an act of physical aggression against any neighbour—anywhere in the world."

Franklin D. Roosevelt

"My fellow citizens of the world: ask not what America will do for you, but what together we can do for the freedom of man."

John F. Kennedy

"When words lose their meaning, people lose their freedom."

Confucius

"People hardly ever make use of the freedom which they have – for example freedom of thought; instead, they demand freedom of speech as a compensation."

Soren Kierkegaard

"In one sense, we are freer now than then. There is far more tolerance for unconventional behaviour, less antisemitism, and less prejudice against blacks and Catholics. In another sense, we are less free. We are close to being enmeshed in that 'network of petty, complicated rules that are both minute and uniform' that Tocqueville conjectured might be the inevitable effect of an excessive drive to equality. There doubtless are many causes for the loss of freedom, but surely a major cause has been the growth of government and its increasing control of our lives. Today, government, directly or indirectly, controls the spending of as much as half our national income."

Milton Friedman

"I liked this country where everyone goes out of his way to meet those who are passing through and throws the doors wide open. I liked this boundless country."

François Mitterand on the United States of America

"Liberty is more important than equality, with which it is incompatible."

Raymond Mortimer

"No amount of political freedom will satisfy the hungry masses."

Lenin

"Freedom is indivisible, and when one man is enslaved, all are not free."

John F. Kennedy

"Freedom gives birth to suffering, while the refusal to be free diminishes suffering. Freedom is not easy, as its enemies and slanderers allege: freedom is hard; it is a heavy burden. Men often renounce freedom to ease their lot."

Nicolai Berdyaev

"The most tremendous thing granted to man is choice, freedom."

Soren Kierkegaard

"'Learn to be free': freedom cannot simply be assumed; it has to be learnt. Suppose that you ask me, 'Can you play the violin?' and I reply, 'I don't know. I've never tried.' You might feel that there was something odd about my answer. Unless I have learnt to play the violin through the exacting discipline of a musical training, I am not free to play Beethoven's violin sonatas. And so it is with every form of freedom. Freedom has to be learnt through the ascetic discipline of precise observation and imaginative thinking; and then it needs to be defended with courage and self-sacrifice."

Kallistos Ware

"My freedom only has meaning if I accept the freedom of others."

François Mitterand

"I'd love to have the emotional freedom to be a bad guy."

Arthur Ashe

"If a nation values anything more than freedom, it will lose its freedom; and the irony of it is that if it is comfort or money that it values more, it will lose that too."

W. Somerset Maugham

"In the four Bryn Mawr lectures, he set out the distinction he was later to make famous between positive and negative liberty. Only at this stage, he called them 'liberal' and 'romantic'. Until Rousseau, liberty had always been understood negatively, as the absence of obstacles to courses of thought and action. With Rousseau, and then with the Romantics, came the idea of liberty being achieved when men are able to realise their innermost natures. Liberty became synonymous with self-creation and self-expression. A person who enjoyed negative liberty – freedom of action or thought – might none

the less lack positive liberty, the capacity to develop his or her innermost nature to the full."
Michael Ignatieff on Isaiah Berlin

"With the heart of a boy so whole and free."
Anthony Powell

"Conceived in Grecian thought, strengthened by Christian morality, and stamped indelibly into American political philosophy, the right of the individual against the State is the keystone of our constitution. Each man is free. He is free in thought. He is free in expression. He is free to worship. To us, who have been reared in the American tradition, these rights have become part of our very being. They have become so much a part of our being that most of us are prone to feel that they are rights universally recognised and universally exercised. But the sad fact is that this is not true. They were clearly won for us in the days just past. And there are large sections of the world today where those rights are denied as a matter of philosophy and as a matter of government."

Fredrik Logevall

"We act as though comfort and luxury were the chief requirements of life, when all we need to make us really happy is something to be enthusiastic about."
Charles Kennedy

"If you destroy leisure, you destroy civilisation."
John Kenneth Galbraith

"To be human is the main thing, and that means to be strong and dear, and of good cheer, in spite of and because of everything, for tears are the preoccupation of weakness."
Rosa Luxemburg

"Let every nation know, whether it wishes us well or ill, that we shall pay any price, bear any burden, meet any hardship, support any friend, oppose any foe to assure the survival and success of liberty."
John F. Kennedy

"Only a man who is happy can create happiness in others."
Paulo Coelho

"And it's the riverbank and the evening sun and being newly married that I still remember now when I pick one of them up and glance through it or sniff its cover to find if the smell of crushed grass lingers."
John Carey on his book collection

"A fulfilled life was unthinkable without the highest degree of joy on one side and an equally high degree of suffering on the other."
Thomas Mann

"Do not believe oh child of man that your happiness is in wishes fulfilled; it lies in duty alone."
Lucie Warburg

"All beginnings are delightful, the threshold is the place to pause."
Goethe

A QUOTATION COLLECTION

"There are three things which are real:
God, human folly and laughter.
The first two are beyond our comprehension
So we must do what we can with the third."

Aubrey Menen

"If it is happiness you want, change yourself, not other people. It is easier to protect your feet with shoes than to carpet the whole world."

Anonymous Greek philosopher

"Grow old with me. The best is yet to be."

Robert Browning

"With whom can I retrace the laughing parts of my life?"

Unattributed

Happiness is "as the multiplicity of agreeable consciousness."

Samuel Johnson

"Happiness is no laughing matter."

Archbishop Richard Whately

"Joy is sometimes a blessing, but it is often a conquest. Our magic moment helps us to change and sends us off in search of our dreams."

Paulo Coelho

"I look forward to a leisure hour with pleasurable agitation – it's so difficult to choose between writing, reading, painting, bricklaying and three or four other things I want to do."

Winston Churchill

"The Chatwins had a firm sense of their place. They were honourable sitters and servers: lawyers, architects, button makers, builders who stayed put. If they strayed it was to bring back and make Birmingham better."
Nicholas Shakespeare

"Oliver Franks believed (Ernest) Bevin had the power of right judgement, which Socrates considered to be the highest virtue."
Andrew Adonis

"Every time in your life you have an opportunity to do right, you should be thankful. For a person to know what is right and then not do it, that would be a sin. Doing the right thing is most important. It lets you have peace. In my opinion, every time you are lucky enough to be given the opportunity to do something right, you shouldn't pass it up."
George Bush (senior)

"Nothing is really ours until we share it."
C.S. Lewis

"The first of all Shakespeare's virtues was mercy, and forgiveness should follow. Judge not that ye be not judged."
Noel Annan

"He who would do good to another must do it in minute particulars; general good is the plea of the scoundrel, hypocrite, and flatterer, for art and science cannot exist in minutely organised particulars."
William Blake

"Silence, it has been said, is a virtue which renders us agreeable to our fellow creatures."
Lord Byron

"The phobia of idleness, the sense of time's winged chariot hurrying near, the conviction that rationality and 'good' values are in fact abnormal in history, and yet the invincible refusal to accept ultimately the consequences of this conviction."
Hugh Trevor-Roper

"Know you are bound to help all who are wronged."
Euripides

"The first thing that I covet for you is a sense of duty. I know that that is a very drab and old-fashioned thing to talk about: duty is lacking in glamour, and it doesn't appear much in the headlines, and the people who make most money are perhaps not always those who value duty most highly. But it is a simple fact of experience that the world is kept going by men who have a sense of obligation. They make civilisation possible, they maintain the fabric of the world and it is on their backs that the line shooters and the glib flashy men in the headlines travel through life. There are two attitudes from which you can choose as you journey though the world. One is summed up in the title of the book: 'The world owes me a living.' The other is summed up as a sense of obligation. It is the people who know that they are debtors to the past, and that they have to repay that debt to the present and the future, who are the salt of the earth and the light of the world, and this value is one of the things that cannot be shaken."
Donald Hughes, Headmaster, Rydal School

"On his death the Methodist Recorder headed his obituary 'Donald Hughes – A Great Headmaster'. Exactly what we mean by great is getting harder to say everyday but in stumbling towards a definition it is no good pointing to this or that virtue or talent. Greatness is an amalgam of many virtues plus a sort of relish which allows one to savour them all at once. And to pretend that greatness admits of no weak spot is to be uncritically blind and thus debase the currency."

Percy Haywood

"You know that I'm happy. You're responsible for my being here today, climbing the mountains of truth, far from my mountains of notebooks and tests. You're making me happy. And happiness is something that multiplies when it is divided."

Paulo Coelho

"Toleration is a necessary consequence of our being human. We are all products of frailty – fallible and prone to error – so let us mutually pardon each other's follies. This is ... the first principle of all human rights."

Voltaire

"If I were to try to read, much less answer, all the attacks made on me, this shop might as well be closed for any other business. I do the very best I can; and I mean to keep doing so until the end. If the end brings me out alright, what is said against me won't amount to anything. If the end brings me out wrong, ten angels swearing I was right would make no difference."

Abraham Lincoln

"Man cannot be whole or dignified until he lives in a community where his private motives lead him to seek the public good."

R.H. Tawney

"Radical changes require adequate authority. A man must have inner strength as well as an influential position. What he does must correspond with higher truth."

Confucius

"Economy of words, economy of effort, economy of expenditure - except when entertaining at home – derived from an uncluttered orderly approach to the routine of life."

Charles Gordon

"In seeking revenge, a man is but equal with his enemy, but in forgiving him, he is superior, for it is a prince's part to pardon."

Francis Bacon

"My own centre of belief, as I matured and grew curious about these things, moved towards the great Gospel of St Matthew, chapter 25 especially, in which he calls us to care for the least of those amongst us, and feed the hungry, clothe the naked, give drink to the thirsty, welcome the stranger, visit the imprisoned. It's enormously significant to me that the only description in the Bible about salvation is tied to one's willingness to act on behalf of one's fellow human beings. The ones who will be deprived of salvation – the sinners – are those who've turned away from their fellow men. People responsive to the great human condition, and who have tried to alleviate its misery – these will be the ones who will join Christ in Paradise."

Edward Kennedy

Truth, Beauty and Art

"Ye shall know the truth and the truth shall make you free."
John 8:32

"Truth emerges from the clash of adverse opinions."
Bhimrao Ranji Ambedkar

"God offers to every mind its choice between truth and repose. Take which you please – you can never have both."
Ralph Waldo Emerson

"The artist does not exist to praise 'decent, godless people. Their only monument the asphalt road/And a thousand lost golf-balls.'"
Noel Annan quoting T.S. Eliot

"At times the truth is ruthless."
Averell Harriman

"Facts are not born free and equal."
C.V. Wedgwood

"Oh memory, thou fond deceiver."
Oliver Goldsmith

"In war, truth is the first casualty."
Aeschylus

"Truth is often eclipsed but never extinguished."
Titus Livius

"Speak your truth quietly and clearly; and listen to others, even the dull and ignorant; they too have their story."
Max Ehrmann

"There is no freedom without truth, for freedom is the child of truth."
Roger Scruton

"Nick's passing forces us to reflect on the arbitrary falseness of public reputation."
Margaret Thatcher on the death of Nicholas Ridley

"One could fall back on the fact that it is not a search for the absolute truth because that lies beyond the human condition to obtain, save in a scientific matter where it can be proven unequivocally one way or the other. But the moment you come to human affairs, the fascinating task is not the portrayal of something as black or white, it's the isolation of the infinite shades of grey to the decision-makers – the judge and the juries who are going to reach their verdicts – and you must try to assess what shade of colour they are actually looking at and bring them round to your thinking. So, it is not some search for the absolute truth. It is to obtain a favourable verdict. And if that involves the … appeal to … an occasional prejudice … or preconceived notions … then that appeal may have to be made."

George Carman

"Mrs Ghandi is incapable of telling the truth, even by mistake."

Bruce Chatwin

"Malice, as so often, contains some truth in it."

Noel Annan

"Truth resides where there is faith."

Paulo Coelho

"Truth is as kaleidoscopic as life."

Siegmund Warburg

"To thine own self be true."

Polonius, in *Hamlet* by William Shakespeare

"It requires in these times much more intellect to marshal so much greater a stock of ideas and observations … hence the multitude of thought only breeds increase of uncertainty. Those who should be guides of the rest, see too many sides to every question. They hear so much said and find that so much can be said about everything that they feel no assurance about the truth of anything."

John Stuart Mill

"'My grassroots constituency dances as they pass …' Jack (a tramp) thought, watching a cabbage white flutter helplessly against the backdraught from the car. 'There are deep truths, too deep for them to grasp.'"

Melissa Harrison

"All his business life Clore searched for the truth, and when he found it, no matter what effect his action might have on any person standing in his way he went ahead with quiet ferocity."

Charles Gordon on business tycoon Charles Clore

"Undoubtedly Clore's greatest virtue was his utterly ruthless honesty."

Charles Gordon

"Authenticity is a shady customer – for a state of affairs to be 'authentic' it must correspond to what life (ought) to be like."

Noel Annan

"The beginning of truth is to wonder at things."

Plato

"Truth is the criterion of historical study; but it's compelling motive is poetic. Its poetry consists in its being true."

G.M. Trevelyan

"An abomination unto the Lord, but a very present help in time of trouble."

An anonymous description of lying

"If we have free speech truth will look after itself."

John Milton

"An excuse is worse and more terrible than a lie, for an excuse is a lie guarded."
Pope John Paul II

"I know that good loves truth."
Marie-Elsa Bragg

"It is rarely possible to carry the torch of truth through a crowd without singeing somebody's beard."
Joshua Byrne

"Through the loveliness of nature, through the touch of sun or rain, or the sigh of the shining restlessness of the sea, we feel: 'unworded things and old to our pained heart appeal'."
Unattributed quoting George Meredith

"No other age had 'produced work which was in its own time, so shatteringly and bewilderingly new, as that of the cubists, the Dadaists, the surrealists and Picasso.'"
Noel Annan quoting C.S. Lewis

"This flag of beauty, hung out by the mysterious Universe, to claim the worship of the heart of man, what is it, and what does its signal mean to us? ... Natural beauty is the ultimate spiritual appeal of the Universe, of nature, or of the God of nature, to their nursling man ... It is the 'highest common denominator in the spiritual life of today.'"
G.M. Trevelyan

"It is bluebell time in Kent."
Lord Denning

"If I were ambitious, I would desire no finer epitaph than that it should be said of me, 'He has added a little to the sweetness of the world and a little to its light.'"
Havelock Ellis

"For the dreamer lives between the lines. And you can see it. He tastes the sentences, murmurs them, and looks into the distance."
Unattributed

"Then it may be that there will often come o'er you –
Glimpses of notes, like the catch of a song;
Visions of boyhood shall float them before you,
Echoes of dreamland shall bear them along."
E.E. Bowen

"Trevelyan believed that walking was the best means whereby a man might regain possession of his own soul, by rejoining him in sacred union with nature."
David Cannadine on G.M. Trevelyan

"Persuasion – the highest form of persuasion at any rate – cannot be achieved without a sense of beauty."
Sir Arthur Quiller-Couch

"Curiosity is one thing invincible in nature."
Freya Stark

"Without vision the people perish, and without natural beauty, the English people will perish in the spiritual sense."
G.M. Trevelyan

"The original quality in any man of imagination is imagery. It is a thing like the landscape of his dreams; the sort of world he would wish to make or in which he would wish to wander; the strange flora and fauna of his own secret planet; the sort of thing he likes to think about."

G.K. Chesterton

"The sun was still in bed, but there was a lightness in the sky over the hundred-acre wood."

A.A. Milne

"To look at things in bloom
Fifty springs are little room."

A.E. Housman

"They're the grey of snow clouds waiting to break."

Robert Harris

"All that in this delightful garden grows,
Should happy be, and have immortal bliss."

Edmund Spenser

"The Wordsworthian joy in nature is not dimmed for me by the knowledge that I shall not possess it for ever. We come and pass and are not, but nature remains, the friend of each of us in turn."

G.M. Trevelyan

"Nothing so clarifies the moral sense as a drop of aesthetic sensibility."

Edith Wharton

"I was here (Verdun, France) briefly in March and the quality of the silence then gave an intimation that spring would be late. I am rarely mistaken about such things."

François Mitterand

"The most beautiful things in the world are the most useless; Peacocks and lilies for instance."

John Ruskin

"So here's an end of roaming
On eves when autumns nigh.
The ear too fondly listens
For Summer's parting sighs
And then the heart replies."

A.E. Housman

"The ugliest men loved the most beautiful things."

Bruce Chatwin

"As if some echo from the future was reaching back and whispering in his ear."

Christy Lefteri

"Take rest; a field that has rested gives a beautiful crop."

Ovid

"It is a beauteous evening, calm and free,
The holy time is quiet as a Nun
Breathless with adoration; the broad sun
Is sinking down in its tranquility;
The gentleness of heaven broods o'er the sea."

William Wordsworth

"Art begins with craft and there is not art until craft has been mastered."

Anthony Burgess

"Modernists valued style, experiment, originality and mockery."

Noel Annan

"There was a daimon in me, and in the end its presence proved decisive. It overpowered me … A creative person has little power over his own life. He is not free. He is captive and driven by his daimon."

Carl Jung

"After national parks, coastal footpaths are the greatest gift of post war government to those who still like a raw edge to their softening lives."

G.M. Trevelyan

"Cities are, or can be, man's supreme art form."

Justin Cartwright

Courage, Confidence and Gratitude

"There's a breathless hush in the close tonight –
Ten to make and the match to win –
A bumping pitch and a blinding light
An hour to play and the last man in.
And it's not for the sake of a ribboned coat,
Or the selfish hope of a season's fame,
But his Captain's hand on his shoulder smote –
'Play up! Play up! and play the game!'
The sand of the desert is sodden red, -
Red with the wreck of a square that broke; -
The Gatling's jammed and the Colonel dead,
And the regiment blind with the dust and smoke.
The river of death has brimmed his banks,
And England's far, and Honour a name,
But the voice of a schoolboy rallies the ranks:
'Play up! Play up! and play the game!'
This is the world that year by year,
While in her place the school is set,
Every one of her sons must hear,
And none that hears it dare forget.
This they all with a joyful mind
Bear through life like a torch in flame,

And falling fling to the host behind -,
'Play up! Play up! and play the game!'"
Henry Newbolt

"Success is never final; failure is never fatal. It is the courage to continue that counts."
Winston Churchill

"Everyone admires courage, and the greenest garlands are for those who possess it."
John F. Kennedy

"It is perhaps meaningful that on the way across the Pacific he read John Buchan's memoir, little remembered today, *Pilgrim's Way*, which would become one of his favourite books. A sterling example of English prose it is, among other things, a paean to an age when panache and daring were treasured, when the great and honourable in literature and politics and statecraft were deemed worthy of emulation. In particular, Buchan's depiction of Raymond Asquith, a young Briton of whose glittering promise (his father was Prime Minister) was cut short by his death in the Battle of the Somme in 1916, stirred something in the combat-bound American. 'There are some men whose brilliance in boyhood and early manhood dazzles their contemporaries and becomes a legend. It is not that they are precocious, for precocity rarely charms, but that for every sphere of life they have the proper complement of gifts and finish each stage so that it remains behind them like a satisfying piece of art … He disliked emotion,' Buchan added of Asquith, 'not because he felt lightly but because he felt deeply.' Two decades later, Ted Sorensen would use this phrase to describe John F. Kennedy."

Fredrik Logevall

"It's not the critic who counts, not the man who points out how the strong man stumbled, or where the doer of deeds could have done better. The credit belongs to the man who is actually in the arena; whose face is marred by the blood and the sweat and the dust; who strives valiantly who errs and comes up short again and again; who knows the great enthusiasms, the great devotions, and spends himself in a worthy cause; who at the best, knows in the end the triumph of high achievement, and who, at worst, if he fails, at least fails while daring greatly; so that his place shall never be with those cold and timid souls who know neither victory nor defeat."

Teddy Roosevelt

"We must learn from misfortune the means of future strength."

Winston Churchill

"A golden age of poetry and power
Of which this noonday's the beginning hour."

Robert Frost

"A Japanese destroyer was bearing down on them like some charging skyscraper ... Kennedy turned the wheel, but it was too late ... the Amagiri shied into the starboard bow of the 109 at a twenty degree angle shearing off a portion of the boat then moved on into the night ... 'This is how it feels to be killed' Kennedy thought to himself ... Jack and ten others miraculously survived most of them floating and amid the debris and burning fuel, some of them barely conscious ... half of the wrecked boat stayed afloat ... they knew the wreckage would not stay afloat forever ... when dawn came up we found ourselves under water up to the bow ... they were deep in hostile territory ... 'There's nothing in the book about a situation like this' he said ... He determined they would swim to a coral island that could just be made out on the horizon some miles away, east of Gizo ... Nor could he be sure if sharks were lurking nearby ... they would have to chance it ... Kennedy ordered the most severely hurt crew member, the poorest swimmer to hold on to a two-by-eight foot plank from which they could paddle along ... while he towed the ailing McMahon, holding the strap of the engineers life jacket in his teeth ... Thus began an epic swim across Blackett Straight – in broad daylight, with the enemy close at hand ... Four hours it would last ... Jack would do the breast stroke for ten to fifteen minutes, rest a little while, then resume swimming, all the while reassuring McMahon and the other men that they were getting closer to their destination ... Near sundown they finally made it, reaching the sandy beach of their precious refuge ... no Japanese in sight ... he lay panting, his feet in the water and his head in the sand ... his back throbbed ... When at last he stood up, he vomited on account of the salt water he had swallowed ... Gradually, he and McMahon made their way up the beach and collapsed under a bush as the others neared the island on their plank.

This occurred in World War II after John Kennedy arrived at Espiritu Santo, a Navy staging post in the new Hebrides (now Vanuatu), south of the Solomon Islands. 'I must say as

I look back on it, it was one of the most dramatic moments I have ever seen in my life.' The sheer tropical beauty of the tableau before them – lush green rainforests sloping down to powdery white beaches and turquoise water. Quietly their ship entered the river … Then a little further on "American fighter planes came down and flew over us after which came a final bend into the harbour and the magnificent sight of a large fleet - some twenty destroyers and four cruisers – riding at anchor around the aircraft carrier Saratosa. It really made the hair stand up on the back of your neck … It was so exciting.'"

Fredrick Logevall

"Courage is rightly esteemed the first of human qualities because … it is the quality which guarantees all others."

Winston Churchill

"Someone who understands what courage is and admires it but has not quite the independence to have it."

Eleanor Roosevelt on John F. Kennedy

"One man with courage makes a majority."

Andrew Jackson

"Boldness has power, genius and magic in it."

Goethe

"One cannot be taught courage. Courage is not even imitated, let alone learnt. But a man can be confirmed in it by the evidence of it in others. Courage, moral and intellectual, was what Housman came to represent to me in the two years during which I sat at his feet in the lecture room and the

single year – it was no more – during which we dined at the same High Table."
Enoch Powell

"Who dares wins."
Motto of the Special Air Service

"Talent is absolutely luck. And no question that the most important thing in the world is courage. People worship talent and it's so ridiculous. Talent is something you're born with, like Kareem (Abdul-Jabber) is born tall. That's why so many talented people are shitheels. But courage is everything because life is harsh and cruel. I believe it completely. The two things that I wish are that I had courage, which I don't feel I have, and that I was born with religious faith. Those two things would be great. I'd probably need less courage if I was born with religious faith. But if I was born with those two things, I'd be very far along in the game."
Woody Allen

"As one's fortunes are reduced, one's spirit must expand to fill the void."
Winston Churchill

"My fear that I wouldn't have the courage under the right circumstances always humiliates me when I'm alone with myself. I cannot think of an act that I've done that required courage of any significance. Anytime that I've thought I might have a serious illness I was always reduced to snivelling, petrified anxiety. And I hope I never have to show courage. I hope I'm never passing a situation where two guys are threatening a little old lady and my choice is to intervene or not, because I would be paralyzed."

Woody Allen

"Let not sorrow dim your eye,
Soon shall every tear be dry
Let not fears your course impede,
great your strength, if great your need."

H. Kirke Whyte

"Courage is not a thing to be commanded at will, and nobody pretended that it was."

Maurice Bowra

"If a man hasn't discovered something he will die for, he isn't fit to live."

Martin Luther King

"No experience can be too strange and no task too formidable if a man can link it up with what he knows and loves," and, "We have been shaken out of our smugness and warned of a great peril, and in that warning lies our salvation. The dictators have done us a marvellous service in reminding us of our true values of life."

John Buchan

"Life is mostly froth and bubble,
Two things stand like stone
Kindness in another's trouble
Courage in your own."

Adam Lindsay Gordon

"The essence of life is to fight as if never to die."
Guy de Rothschild

"Avoid the temptation to do anything heroic."
Clifford Mortimer

"Hold fast in adversity, never give in and the Gods will help you."
Goethe

"Let courage rise with danger."
George Duffield.

"Man cannot discover new oceans until he has courage to lose sight of the shore."
Anonymous

"I had no shoes – and I murmured until I met a man who had no feet."
Hindu Proverb

"The war which found the measure of so many men never got to the bottom of him and, when the Grenadiers strode into the crash and thunder of the Somme, he went to his fate, cool, poised, resolute, matter of fact, debonair."
Winston Churchill on Raymond Asquith

"My sword I give to him that shall succeed me in my pilgrimage, and my courage and skill to him that can get it."
John Bunyan

"It is only the last and wildest kind of courage that can stand on a tower before 10,000 people and tell them that twice two is four."

G.K. Chesterton

"It takes courage to face a duellist with a pistol and it takes courage to face a British general with an army. But it takes still greater and far higher courage to face friends with a grievance."

Harry Truman

"Perhaps those, who, trembling most, maintain a dignity in their fate, are the bravest: resolution on reflection is real courage."

Horace Walpole

"If you can meet with Triumph and Disaster,
And treat those two imposters just the same …"

Rudyard Kipling

"The hottest places in hell are reserved for those who, in a period of moral crisis, maintain their neutrality."

Dante

"Great Men, Great Nations, have not been boasters and buffoons, but perceivers of the terror of life, and have manned themselves to face it."

Ralph Waldo Emerson

"There is no doubt that the thing that pays in life is audacity."

John Buchan

"There is nothing in the world so much admired as a man who knows how to bear unhappiness with courage."
Seneca

"So often our experience of courage must be cobbled together by negative inference from those miserable moments in which we wish we had it and found it wanting."
William Miller

"In the act of courage, the most essential part of our being prevails against the less essential."
Paul Tillich

Hero: "A man who exhibits extraordinary bravery, firmness or greatness of soul in connection with any pursuit, work or enterprise; a man admired and venerated for his achievements and noble qualities."
Oxford Shorter English Dictionary

"You can only be brave when you are afraid."
Field Marshall Harding

"He has not learnt the lesson of life who does not every day surmount fear."
Ralph Waldo Emerson

"A rose is for courage."
Marie-Elsa Bragg

"All men dream: but not equally.
Those who dream by night in the dusty recesses of their
Minds wake in the day to find that it was
Vanity; but the dreamers of the day are
dangerous men, for they may act their dream
with open eyes, to make it possible. This I did."

T.E. Lawrence

"Only great men change their minds."

Adlai Stevenson

"The best fashion accessory is confidence."

Vivienne Westwood

"Confidence is a very tender plant. It can wither quickly but may take many long years to recover."

Lewis Whyte

"In business, as in politics, he cautions, a confident pose is crucial. Nobody should look anxious, except those who have no anxiety."

Lionel Rothschild

"In 1960, soon after *The Affluent Society*, I took two friends to stay at the Galbraith's house in New Fane, Vermont. 'Well, we have certainly seen the public squalor on the way here!' one of them said as we bounced up the rough and long dirt road. 'I only hope we see the private affluence when we arrive!' So, I suppose, we did, but only up to a point. For while Ken would never dream of not staying at the Carlyle in this city or the Ritz in London, neither he nor

Kitty has ever believed in changing their domestic lifestyle to keep up with the royalties. That of course is a tribute to their supreme, unaffected and therefore wholly splendid self-confidence."

Roy Jenkins

"Gratitude is the mother of all virtues."

G.K. Chesterton

"What comfort therefore, have we against these losses? This, surely, that we must remember them even after they are lost, and that we must not suffer to fall out of our minds the joy that we have had from them, even though we have them no more. What we have may be snatched from us. But what we have had is ours for ever. Ungrateful indeed is he who, having lost something, does not acknowledge his debt of gratitude for that which he has once possessed."

Seneca

"Gratitude unlocks the door of generosity: We get what we give – when we bless others we are blessed – when we love we are loved – when we give, we greatly receive."

Robert Alan Silverstein

"There's an old joke. Two elderly women are at a Catskill's Mountain resort, and one of them says, 'Boy, the food at this place is really terrible.' The other one says, 'Yeah, and such small portions.' Well, that's essentially how I feel about life. Full of loneliness and misery and suffering and unhappiness, and it's all over much too quickly."

Woody Allen

"Gratitude isn't an emotion – But the expectation of gratitude is a very lively one."

C.P. Snow

Faith, Fate and Hope

"Lord give me the courage to change what I can, the Grace to accept the things I can't, and the wisdom to know the difference."

Reinhold Niebuhr

"If we are not reborn – if we cannot learn to look at life with the innocence and the enthusiasm of childhood – it makes no sense to go on living."

Paulo Coelho

"People are afraid of the infinity of their freedom to do whatever they like with their lives, and so they pretend to themselves that they are bound by unavoidable duties, or by the moral law. A human being stands completely alone and is by himself responsible for his actions. In this way each one of us is a romantic hero. Recognising this essential isolation is a proof of 'authentic existence'; and if there is any room for virtue, in Sartre's theory, authenticity or sincerity, the absence of bad faith is the only one."

Mary Warnock

"They have put it over the head of the judge so that he not be troubled by its sight … They should have placed the image at the other end of the room, so that before pronouncing sentence the judge would have before his eyes the example of judicial error which our civilisation regards as the shame of humanity."

Georges Clemenceau describing an image of the Crucifixion

'Maurice had discovered in the trenches of the Great War that poetry could literally save a personality from disintegration. It gave clues to a beauty of living, a spirituality, that dignified everyday events. It suggested that life may have a purpose after all.'

Leslie Mitchell on Maurice Bowra

'The poet was the most blessed of all men. Endowed with special talents he is privileged to have special insights. The Gods spoke thought poets, in order to warn, to instruct and to edify. As a result, an intimate connection between poetry and prophecy was set up. As Bowra put it, "the poet is wife because he has a special knowledge." After all poets and prophets have much in common.'

Leslie Mitchell

"The last thing is this. Last month a distinguished historian was speaking in a television programme. He is not known as a particularly religious man in the orthodox sense, but he said something about religion which I thought very helpful. He defined it as 'feeling pretty humble before the mystery'. I should hate to think that anyone could leave here unaware of the mystery – that he could go through life satisfied with a narrow little materialism, with both feet on the ground, and both eyes on the main chance, and no sense of eternity in his soul. There are times in life when we encounter beauty in Nature or in Art, or goodness in character or in action, and we hear somewhere (not with our ears) and we are aware of another dimension, the accents of an unknown idiom, the voice of Truth, incoherent but unmistakable – you can grow very insensitive to that sort of experience unless it is part of your way of life; one of the things that cannot be shaken."

Donald Hughes, Headmaster, Rydal School

"I do not believe it is possible to sustain the will to change the world, on however small a scale, without some faith which goes beyond the world as seen by science alone."

Denis Healey

"They (the words in Psalm 19) suggest a union of reason and instinct of faith; and surely reason rightly attuned by humility and sympathy is the best instrument we have for the appreciation of whatever the truth may be."

Mary Warnock

"The clouds you so much dread
Are big with mercy and shall break
In blessings on your head."

William Cowper

"From now on it is only through a conscious choice and through a deliberate policy that humanity can survive."

Pope John Paul II

"You must do what you think you cannot do."

Teddy Roosevelt

"Just as you and I are physically changing all the time and yet remaining the same people, so we need a faith and a way which is always changing and yet always remains the same thing. Where do you expect to find it? This is what the doctrine of the Holy Spirit is about."

James D.G. Dunn

"I am the way, the Truth and the Life. I am the Alpha and Omega, the beginning and the end. Jesus Christ, the same yesterday, today and forever."

John 14:6

"Weakness, moral sickness and our crying need of salvation are not barriers between ourselves and God. They provide bonds which unite us to him. In the spiritual lives of many people fear dominates, not love. Life built on fear is built on the wrong foundations."

Cardinal Basil Hume

"And though the Lord give you the bread of adversity and the water of affliction yet shall not thy teachers be removed into a corner anymore, but thine eyes shall see thy teachers."

Isaiah 30:19-20

"This world is not conclusion
A sequel lies beyond."

Emily Dickinson

"There is something about us, that knows better often what we would be at than we ourselves."

Henry Moore

"My own view is that mankind has somehow lost touch with the spiritual forces that guide our species, but that many individuals remain in touch with their 'something that knows better what we would be at'."

William Rees-Mogg

"There's a divinity that shapes our ends, Rough-hew them how we will."

William Shakespeare

"In the past the prophetic voice to which I have become accustomed has always been my constant companion, opposing me in even quite trivial things if I was going to take the wrong course."

Socrates

"From the darkest corners of our ego it directs our veritable life, the one that is not to die, and pays no heed to our thought or to anything emanating from our reason, which believes that it guides our steps."

Maurice Maeterlinck

"God gives us everlasting life. Here we move from the finite to the infinite and since we have only the language of the finite at our disposal it is unprofitable to speculate or to talk too much about it. 'In my father's house are many mansions; if it were not so I would have told you. I go to prepare a place for you.' That is enough for us. We aren't meant to peer inquisitively into the future like a weak-minded reader peering into the last chapter of the book and missing the experiences which the author intended for him. Life is to be

lived in the present tense: we know enough about the future to live, if we will, in complete trust and confidence."
Donald Hughes, Headmaster, Rydal School

"Churchill was once referred to as a pillar of the Church – 'No No,' he replied, 'not a pillar of the Church but a buttress, supporting it from the outside.'"
Also attributed to William Temple

"Neglect not the gift that is within thee."
Timothy 4:14

"The peace which passeth all understanding."
Christopher Mayhew

"The World endures but an hour, spend it in devotion."
Inscribed on a Wall of the Taj Mahal

"The World is a bridge; pass over it, but build no house thereon."
Hazrat Isa

"Autumn even more than Spring, is a crossing of the line; an embarkation point for a journey of the mind. Even at Durham, in Europe's greatest Romanesque masterpiece, you need to believe nothing save the infinite, creative genius of your own species. Faith comes in many forms, and there is no better time than autumn to refresh it. 'Look,' as Ian Nairn would have said, 'and think on.'"
Richard Girling

"One child lost to the faith usually becomes a family lost to the faith, and not many generations later a whole community of unbelief is set in motion because of some earlier neglect of parental duties."
Carl F.H. Henry

"Western thought is governed by a binary system: we look at problems in two ways, from their positive and negative sides. From this, we achieve a synthesis and resolve the issue. But this simplistic materialistic approach swears against our innermost natures, because humankind, whether we recognise it or not, is trinitarian. If this were not the case, we would not have differences of opinion since we would all be programmed by a common logic. However, this patently is not the case. While a computer produces the identical answers given the same inputs by a Japanese, an American or a Frenchman, we know that the point of view of these three nationalities in their daily lives (which surmounts logical truth) is very different.

Logic then is binary, but there are elements in humans which defy logic. As Christ remarked 'Man does not live by bread alone' and it is spirits and beliefs which make man trinitarian. Pre-renaissance man was trinitarian. His beliefs were spiritually orientated, for his soul was focused on God and logic was the servant to his soul. Today, however, the West having sacrificed God to reason, logic is dominant and is in conflict with man's soul. On a personal level western society is dislocated and neurotic; on a national level it is disorganised and chaotic. This is the inevitable result of spiritual neglect.

Kant made it crystal clear in his preface to the second edition of the Critique that, far from destroying the belief in God, his purpose was to make belief possible: 'I must, therefore, abolish knowledge to make room for belief. The dogmatism of metaphysics is the true source of unbelief (always dogmatic) which militates against morality.'"

Denis Healey

"It always signifies to me the abandonment of what I am about to do."

Socrates describing his inner spiritual voice

"Give the Jesuits his soul, she may have reasoned, and they will give him a brain."

John Le Carré in *The Secret Pilgrim*

"Ayer addressed the genuinely philosophical arguments which claim that the Universe must, as a matter of logic, have had a creator. Ayer in fact denied, in true positivist fashion, that any sense could be made of an entity existing outside space and time, on the grounds that 'in being made to transcend time, it loses all possibility of being, even in principle, accessible to our experience'. But even if the existence of such a being was intelligible, deistic arguments for its existence plainly were not. The suggestion, for instance, that God must have caused the universe, 'argument from design', rather than proving the existence of God."

Anthony Kenny on A.J. Ayer

"Get religion like a Methodist. Experience it like a Baptist. Be sure of it like a Disciple. Stick to it like a Lutheran. Conciliate it like a Congregationalist. Be proud of it like an Episcopalian. Simplify it like a Quaker. Glorify it like a Jew. Pay for it like a

Presbyterian. Practice it like a Christian Scientist. Work at it like the Salvation Army. Propagate it like a Roman Catholic. Enjoy it like a Negro."

Edgar Dewitt Jones

"But it was King's College Chapel which, during these years of early adolescence, provided for me my most meaningful religious experience. Evensong was sung at half-past three on Sundays and in the evening on weekdays, and I would often drop in when cycling home from school. I can recall the solemnity, the grandeur and the beauty of the building, the high, soaring magnificence of the roof, the candle-lit gloom, the decorous procession of the boys in the choir, the order and the beauty of the traditional service. This, I believed then and still do believe, was what worship should be. I think I probably realised even then that I was in danger of confusing worship of God with a strong emotional and aesthetic response to architecture, music and literature but it seemed to me that religion could be an aesthetic experience, and that God should be worshipped in the beauty of holiness."

P.D. James

"He recognised that Christianity is a religion that sits in judgement on this world."

Noel Annan on Enoch Powell

"God only wills for us what we would will for ourselves if we knew as much as He knows."

St Cuthbert's Parish Magazine

"Man has made mathematics, but God reality."
William Butler Yeats

"Tis not the object, but the light
That maketh heav'n."
Thomas Traherne

"God is cunning, but he is not malevolent."
Albert Einstein

"If in the hurry of business and cares of the world I forget thee, do not thou Oh God forget me."
Charles Churchill

"Where others see the dawn coming over the hill, I see the sons of God shouting for joy."
William Blake

"A child is not likely to find a father in God unless he finds something of God in his father."
Glen Wheeler

"If we are to have a religion, it should be one that recognises the true importance of a single moment in time, the instant when you are fully and completely alive."
John Mortimer

"The force that through the green fuse drives the flower."
Dylan Thomas

"Traditionalism may also lie behind an approach to Islam (by Prince Charles) that is significantly more sympathetic than is normal in British public life."
Catherine Mayer

"We were the tops at everything, especially humility."
Tony O'Reilly

"The General had the terrified child stripped naked and made to run. Then the hounds were released, hunted him down, and tore him to pieces. Christians are bound to forgive the General. They must forgive everyone. He acknowledges that forgiveness is necessary if the world is to attain divine harmony. But for him the suffering of the innocent is too much to pay for divine harmony and he wants no part of it."
John Carey

"When one has this terrible temptation to ask 'Why, oh why?' how terrible must have been the temptation of those simple men who, after the apparent utter failure – of the whole campaign, ending in the meanest possible form of death, by assassination on a cross – somehow managed to get a faith to carry them on …"
Harold Macmillan

"Recite the Beatitudes and you will see that they cannot be applied to the world of affairs: they are God's judgement on that world and its pretensions. Religion helps to reconcile man to the pains of mortality and the dissonances of life. Faith is a voice that does not speak in the same language

as other forms of experience. But Religion is no more than another voice."
Noel Annan

"The Christian Faith has not been tried and found wanting. It has been found difficult and left untried."
G.K. Chesterton

"It's not what you've done but what you are that matters."
Len Cragg, Vicar of Saint Cuthbert's Church, Lytham

"Now is not the time to make enemies."
Voltaire, being asked to renounce Satan on his deathbed

"Belief, as so often happens, was pleasantly disassociated from thought."
Kenneth Galbraith

"Science can purify religion from error and superstition. Religion can purify science from idolatry and false absolutes."
Pope John Paul II

"Can there be a natural instinct for good behaviour, like a belief in natural justice, and if so does it matter if it shines from a divine light or has evolved from the human instinct of mutual aid? The point at which beliefs meet may be more significant, more useful to contemplate, than their sources."
John Stuart Mill

"Once you have embarked upon the impossible concept of God, you will know that real love permits no rejection.

Perhaps that is something only a sinner can properly understand. Only a sinner knows the scale of God's forgiveness."

John Le Carré

"The very best of luck, you always have it because you deserve it."

Xan Smiley

"All of us, I suggest, choose religious beliefs that meet our imaginative needs, and it is because they meet our imaginative needs that we choose them."

John Carey

"Our Lord was a young man throughout his ministry, and He was still a young man when they crucified Him. People thought many things about Him, but no one ever thought Him stuffy or respectable. If He appeared among us today with the same teaching, it would still strike people as new. What would we think of a man who told us to treat our enemies and our friends in exactly the same way: how many of us agree with that? … that the true measure of success was the number of people whom we could serve: is that your idea of success? Who told very bad people that they were forgiven when they did no more than say that they were sorry, and very good people that they could not be forgiven because they were unforgiving?"

Donald Hughes, Headmaster, Rydal School

"Lord, dismiss us with Thy blessing;
Thanks for mercies past receive;

Pardon all, their faults confessing;
Time that's lost may all retrieve."
Henry James Buckoll

"There lives more faith in honest doubt."
Alfred, Lord Tennyson

"I deny nothing but doubt everything."
Byron

"If one turns all one's strength to something, in the end everything comes out for the best."
Lucie Warburg

"The afternoon knows what the morning never suspected."
Swedish proverb

"If you don't believe in God, all you have to believe in is decency … decency is very good. Better decent than indecent. But I don't think it's enough?"
Harold Macmillan

"Twelve days before I was given the statutes, keys and seal of Oxford, I had lost the Glasgow travel warrants and rights of admission to the House of commons, it was a good lesson in the even-handedness of fate."
Roy Jenkins

"A Jew never returns to a place of misfortune."
Jacques Attali

"Men had always understood there were impersonal forces beyond their control that governed their fate."
Noel Annan

"I do not believe in fate or in inevitable disaster."
François Mitterand

"If we look back on our past life, we shall see that one of its most usual experiences is that we have been helped by our mistakes and injured by our most sagacious decisions."
Winston Churchill

"One Doctor to another: 'About the termination of pregnancy – I want your opinion. The father was syphilitic. The mother tuberculous. Of the children born the first was blind, the second died, the third was deaf and dumb and the fourth was tuberculous. What would you have done?' 'I would have ended the next pregnancy.' 'Then you would have murdered Beethoven.'"
Maurice Baring

"Our lives, as Miriam (Rothschild) said, are shaped long before we are born; tendrils of DNA, ancestral history and behavioural traits are embedded into every part of our being."
Hannah Rothschild

"To be uncertain is uncomfortable; but to be certain is ridiculous."
Goethe

"I could have. What does this phrase mean? At any given moment in our lives, there are certain things that could have happened but didn't. The magic moments go unrecognised, and then suddenly, the hand of destiny changes everything."

Paulo Coelho

"Old men plant trees."

A Somerset Farmer

"Man was made for Joy and Woe:
And when this we rightly know
Thro' the World we safely go."

William Blake

"Hope is necessary in every existence."

Samuel Johnson

"Never be pessimistic. Pessimism is a sickness you treat like any other sickness."

Aristotle Onassis

"In circa 1946 Jack Kennedy spoke at the annual Boston Independence Day oration on the topic of 'Some Elements of the American Character' – pointing to the vital role played by religions and idealistic conviction in the nation's history including in the eradication of slavery and in the recent victory over Nazi Germany and imperial Japan, he warned his audience that moral conviction alone was never enough; a healthy dose of pragmatic realism would be required as well. Thus, in World War II, the idealism with which he had entered the battle made the subsequent disillusionment all the more bitter and revealed a dangerous fact to this element of the American character, for this bitterness, a direct result of our inflated hopes, brought a radical change in our foreign policy and a resulting withdrawal from Europe. We failed to make the adjustment between what we had hoped to win and what we actually could win. Our idealism was too strong. We would not compromise."

Fredrik Logevall

"'Would you tell me, please, which way I ought to go from here?' she asked. 'That depends a good deal on where you want to get to,' said the cat."

Lewis Carroll in *Alice's Adventures in Wonderland*

"It is not necessary to hope in order to undertake. It is not necessary to succeed in order to persevere."

William the Silent

"Hope is a story of shattered dreams."

Martin Luther King

"You see things and you say 'why?' I dream of things that never were and say, 'why not?'

George Bernard Shaw

"Most people get beaten back by life, but your support helped me stubbornly hold on to the dreams I had."

James Rebanks to his grandfather

"The English Language is the richest in the word in monosyllables. Four words of one syllable each … contain salvation, for this country and the whole world, and they are Faith, Hope, Love and Work. No government in this country today which has no faith in the people, hope in the future, love for its fellowmen, and will not work and work, and work, will ever bring this country through into better days and better times, or will ever bring Europe through or the world through."

Stanley Baldwin

"And not by eastern windows only,
When daylight comes, comes in the light,
In front the sun climbs slow, how slowly,
But westward look, the land is bright."

A.H. Clough

Success, Failure and Effort

"If one wants to be successful, one must think; one must think until it hurts."

Lord Thomson

"If I have seen further, it is by standing on the shoulders of Giants."

Isaac Newton

"In the field of observation, chance favours the mind that is prepared."

Louis Pasteur

"Without contraries there is no progression."

William Blake

"There is a Spanish proverb to the effect that the shock that does not kill you makes you."

Jennie Erdal

"Above all, *The Shepherd's Life* is freighted with personal discovery. It is about Rebanks testing himself against the outside world, against the academic system, against the weather and against more seasoned shepherds. It is about finding one's true "alive and necessary" self. It is about how the countryside can battle to keep its traditions alive. "

The *Sunday Times* on **James Rebanks**

"A man may labour for a professional lifetime, especially in sport or battle, but posterity needs a single transcendental event to fix him in permanent memory. Every man must be a Wellington on the right side of his personal Waterloo; detractors will argue for ever about the general quality of your life and work, but they can never erase an event."

Stephen Jay Gould

By the standards of Rembrandt or Picasso there is no visual artist of genius; by the standards of Aeschylus or Shakespeare no poet of genius; by the standards of Charlemagne or of Abraham Lincoln no statesman of genius, not in the whole wide world. It is as though the collective daemons had 'been silenced' – yet I do not believe that the individual daemon has lost a voice."

William Rees-Mogg

"The language we use when immersed in the world of affairs is the mode of practical experience. It is neither more nor less important a mode than poetry, history or science; but most of us use it more often. Whether or not we know it, we speak this language whenever we exert our will. To act is to exert our will. Each of us in society try to get pleasure, or love someone, or find God, or rule others, or find solitude. Each one of us tries to change our present state into a more agreeable state and hence, in doing so, we encounter others whose desire and activities may frustrate or conflict with ours. The only way to avoid such frustrations and conflict is for everyone to submit to the same rules."

Noel Annan

"The most successful man in life is the man who has the best information."

Lionel Rothschild

"The penalty of success is to be bored by people who used to snub you."

Nancy Astor

"Meyer owed his success as an advice giver to the same two qualities that made him such a unique investor: an ability to cold bloodedly dissect opportunities, problems and personalities; and the iron determination to follow through and get what he and his client wanted."

William N. Thorndike on Robert Meyer

"Those who carry on great public schemes must be proof against the worst delays, the most mortifying disappointments, the most shocking of insults and, which is worst of all, the presumptuous judgements of the ignorant on their designs."

Edmund Burke

"You don't have to be great to start, but you have to start to be great."

Zig Ziglar

"Experience and observation have convinced me that we learn most when faced with a real problem which we are obliged to solve. These are the circumstances in which we give of our best and in which we are prepared to listen more acutely to the people around us."
Arnold Weinstock

"Public opinion is everything. With it nothing can fail, without it nothing can succeed."
Abraham Lincoln

"Do not judge me by my successes, judge me by how many times I fell down and got back up again."
Nelson Mandela

"Self-control, with simplicity and integrity (not pride, but I will not say humility), must be my aim. Or else I shall not achieve what I want to achieve."
A.L. Rowse

"I understand for the first time that our sense of belonging is all about participation."
James Rebanks

"People are either hard on themselves or pleased with themselves. The former are those who make the world better. He who accepts higher challenges and who succumbs in the end in his effort to take up these challenges is the real victor in life."
Siegmund Warburg

"On the whole it is not good that human nature should have the road of life made too easy. Better to be under the necessity of working hard and faring meanly than to have everything done ready to hand and a pillow of down to repose upon."
Samuel Smiles

"I believe in getting into hot water – it helps keep you clean."
G.K. Chesterton

"It seems to me that obligations and responsibilities come first, and only when the citizen has faithfully discharged them is he justified in claiming rights and liberties and privileges. I believe that our way of life would be more agreeable if we got the sequence right."
Henry Benson

"A crank is a man with a new idea – until it catches on."
Mark Twain

"One of the most important things in life is to be lucky with your bad luck."
Barbara Castle

"If I had to choose between someone who had great talent but was short on grit and desire, and another player who was good but had great determination and drive, I would always prefer the latter."
Alex Ferguson

"I don't think a nation can live without religion. I don't find a man who could … if you don't pray every night, and if you don't believe in God, and if you don't think you can serve God eventually, you can't solve those problems and you can't even then survive them, I don't think. And so that's my philosophy of life – there are neither successes or failures, you do your best, and that's life."

Harold Macmillan

"Why hadn't I done better? I had a brain but why was I so stupid? He admired me in some way but why didn't I grow up and fulfil myself."

Charles Clore on Charles Gordon

"Nothing is so exhausting as indecision, and nothing is so futile."

Bertrand Russell

"If you do what you've always done, you'll get what you've always gotten."

Anonymous

"Where there is no vision, the people perish."

Proverbs 29:18

"Don't get mad, get even."

Joe Kennedy

"Heaven help the man who does his best and fails, there is no other hope, and I have no other use for him."

Woodrow Wilson

"I have a fear of failure – I don't like to let anybody down. That's a thing that worries me – that I might make a bad job of something, or that somebody who was relying on me might find that that was unjustified."

Arnold Weinstock

"There was the neo-Keynesian nanny who said you should feed a cold and the monetarist nanny who said you should starve it. Whatever course you chose, it was obvious that once you get set on a particular doctrine and ceased to be pragmatic, that was the end of you."

Harold Macmillan

"To lose face in Japan is to lose everything. But to lose everything is not necessarily to lose face."

Leonard Mosley

"Nobody is despised by other people unless he has first lost respect for himself."

Seneca

"The best thing going for me was that I had nothing to lose."

James Rebanks

"The human mind cannot operate lucidly and with genius in the atmosphere of a committee."

Solly Zuckerman

"The way to win battles, wars, games is by attacking."

Alex Ferguson

"If it had not been for these things, I might have lived out my life talking at street corners to scorning men. I might have died, unmarked, unknown, a failure. Now we are not a failure. This is our career and our triumph. Never in our full life could we hope to do such work for tolerance, for justice, for man's understanding of man as now we do by accident. Our words – our lives – our pains – nothing! The taking of our lives – lives of a good shoemaker and a poor fish-peddler – all! That last moment belongs to us – that agony is our triumph."

Bartolomeo Vanzetti

"I know you will think I am paranoid, but that machine knows me!"

John McEnroe

"Never take anything for granted."

Oscar Wilde

"Neutrality can serve wrong."

Possibly Eleanor Roosevelt

"You have to be prepared to fail if you want to succeed."

Martha Lane Fox

"Once you say farewell to discipline you say goodbye to success and set the stage for anarchy."

Alex Ferguson

"Failure, even if delivered by an apparently irrevocable event, stimulates his fighting spirit. This is how he has been able to restore a number of situations which would have been lost for other people."

Pierre Haas on Siegmund Warburg

"We become authorities and experts in the practical and scientific spheres by so many separate acts and hours of work. If anyone keeps faithfully busy each hour of the working day, he may safely leave the final result to itself. He can with perfect certainty count on waking up some fine morning to find himself one of the competent ones of his generation … silently, between all the details of his business, "the power of judging" … will have built itself up within him."

William James

"Whatever you can do or dream you can … begin it."

Goethe

"Perseverance is favourable."

From the *I Ching*

"Nothing in the world can take the place of persistence. Talent will not; genius will not; education will not. Persistence and determination alone are omnipotent."

Calvin Coolidge

"Those who rest on their laurels find themselves sitting on a thorn bush."

Unattributed

"You don't fail until you give up trying."

Aristotle Onassis

SUCCESS, FAILURE AND EFFORT

"The first reason was my own obstinate will to carry on in the face of adversity, one of the many habits of discipline that my father instilled in me and all of my brothers and sisters. We were taught never to give up, never to passively accept fate, but to exhaust every last ounce of will and hope in the face of any challenges. "

Edward Kennedy

"Work is the grand cure of all the maladies that ever test mankind."

Thomas Carlyle

Charles Dickens' philosophy of life "Action, usefulness … the determination to be of service – we must all be up and doing something."

Paul Johnson

"In the last resort, it is only by doing things that we learn what can be done."

Arnold Weinstock

"This is the greatest lesson a child can learn. It is the greatest lesson anyone can learn. It is the greatest lesson I have learned: if you persevere, stick with it, work at it, you have a real opportunity to achieve something. Sure, there will be storms along the way. And you might not reach your goal right away. But if you do your best and keep a time compass, you'll get there."

Edward Kennedy

"This idea embraces the whole man, recognising and accepting virtues and vices, heroism and failure. Completeness of living necessitates each man being free to make mistakes, and he will make many, but he can follow his own star and his own soul and find his full being both in his own likeness to other men and his difference from them. Nearly everyone would fail in this strenuous endeavour, but the Greeks saw small heroisms in the striving."

Maurice Bowra

"During the Lewinsky affair – 'There was nothing I (Bill Clinton) could do about that, but I could do my job every day, and so I got up and concentrated on the things that I could impact instead of being consumed by the things I had no impact on.' He knew he'd done wrong. He also knew the campaign against him was overdone, and he trusted people to see that too."

Alastair Campbell

"Idleness leads to languor, and languor to disgust."

Henri-Frédéric Amiel

"The people I admire are those that have constancy of purpose. I'm in awe of people who put their back out to be as good as they can be."

David Yarrow

"Until you try, you don't know what you can't do."

Henry James

SUCCESS, FAILURE AND EFFORT

"The heights by great men reached and kept
Were not attained by sudden flight
But they, while their companions slept,
Were toiling upward in the night."

Henry Wadsworth Longfellow

Risk, Caution and Conformity

"Pitiful is the person who is afraid of taking risks. Perhaps this person will never be disappointed or disillusioned; perhaps she won't suffer the way people do when they have a dream to follow. But when that person looks back – and at some point, everyone looks back – she will hear her heart saying, 'What have you done with the miracles that God planted in your days? What have you done with the talents God bestowed on you? You buried yourself in a cave because you were fearful of losing those talents. So, this is your heritage: the certainty that you wasted your life.'"

Paulo Coelho

"Risk is probability times impact."

Victoria Glendinning

"Not a change for the better in our human housekeeping has ever taken place that wise and good men have not opposed it – have not prophesied that the world would wake up to find its throat cut in consequence."

James Russell Lowell

"You have to take risks for what you believe to be right."
Martin Luther King

"A life during which you have caused no offence would be as blandly uneventful as death itself. Being caused offence stirs up the spirits, summons up the blood and starts the adrenalin flowing. A political or religious belief which can't stand up to insult, mockery and abuse is not worth having."
John Mortimer

"Our patience will achieve more than our force."
Edmund Burke

"I'm not interested in what we can make, I'm only interested in what we can lose. The downside risk is something that I constantly hammer home to any of my people involved in a smaller way in acquisitions. I say, 'Don't worry about how much you can make, how much can you lose?'"
Gordon White

"An opportunity never presents itself twice, and that settles everything."
Siegmund Warburg

"Beware of the lust to finish."
Donald English

"Don't ever take a fence down until you know the reason why it was put up."
G.K. Chesterton

"Never begin a deal, a battle or a love affair if the fear of losing overshadows the prospect of winning."

Aristotle Onassis

"He that has a secret should not hide it but hide that he has it to hide."

Thomas Carlyle

"Getting out of a situation or getting into something, the secret is always to move at the right speed."

Aristotle Onassis

"Society ... practices a tyranny more formidable than many kinds of political oppression, since ... it leaves fewer means of escape, penetrating much more deeply into the details of life, and enslaving the soul itself ... there needs protection also against the tyranny of the prevailing opinion and feeling."

John Stuart Mill

"Routine is fine,
Blessing is grace,
The two together,
Prevents haste."

Unattributed

"And if we have censorship which stops us offending anymore, the truth may be concealed in the surrounding blur."

John Mortimer

Time, Travel and Change

"The lights begin to twinkle from the rocks:
The Long Day wanes: the slow moon climbs: the deep
Moans round with many voices. Come, my friends,
Tis not too late to seek a newer world."

Tennyson

"Tempus Edax Rerum." (Time the devourer of everything).

Ovid

"I had become, with the approach of night once more aware of loneliness and time – those two companions without whom no journey can yield us anything."

Lawrence Durrell

"The less one has to do, the less time one finds to do it."

Jim Rohn

"Past has gone – Future hasn't arrived. The now is a gift that's why it's called the present."

Anonymous

"Take your hats off to the past but take your coats off to the future."

Clare Booth Luce

"Don't let it be forgot
That once there was a spot
For one brief shining moment
That was known as Camelot."

Alan Jay Lerner

"We talked late into the night, arguing whether or not we, too, have journeys mapped out in our central nervous systems; it seemed the only way to account for our insane restlessness."

Joyce Khan

"Gradually the idea for a book began to take shape. It was to be wildly ambitious and intolerant work, a kind of 'Anatomy of Restlessness' that would enlarge on Pascal's dictum about the man sitting quietly in a room. The argument, roughly, was as follows: that in becoming human, man had acquired, together with his straight legs and striding walk, a migratory 'drive' or instinct to walk long distances through the seasons; that this 'drive' was inseparable from his central nervous system; and that, when warped in conditions of settlement, it found outlets in violence, greed, status seeking or a mania for the new. This would explain why mobile societies such as the gypsies are egalitarian, thing-free and resistant to change; also why, to re-establish the harmony of the First State, all the great teachers – Buddha, Lao-tse, St Francis – had set the perpetual pilgrimage at the heart of their message and told their disciples, literally, to follow The Way."

Bruce Chatwin

"Such moments (discovery of man's first experimentation with fire) come to you in remote places. It's as if the curtain that separates us from a broader vision is briefly lifted. We're tied to a sequential time sequence, it's the only way evolution can work – otherwise everything happens at once. But every now and then the process falters and we look through a chink at, I suppose, the eternity religious speak of. When this happens, it's such a startling experience that you hanker after it when you're back in the world of sequence. I think that's what Chatwin did when he returned to the sequential world, he found it tiresome and set off on another expedition."

Bob Brain on Bruce Chatwin

"In choosing the Welsh border, Bruce returned to the area he loved best. 'No man can wander in fact without a base,' he said in 1984. 'You have to have a sort of magic circle to which you belong. It's not necessarily where you were born or where you were brought up. It's somewhere you identify with, to which you always happen to go back. This area of the Welsh border I regard as one of the emotional centres of my life … It's what Proust calls the soil on which I still may build.'"

Nicholas Shakespeare on Bruce Chatwin

"Bruce's theory about people moving because movement is a natural condition is wrong. I've spent lots and lots of time with lots of groups. All say it's nice to move on; you don't have quarrels you get in villages or cities; you go to pretty places, you get up in the cool mountains in summer and the plains in winter."

Jeremy Swift on Bruce Chatwin

"The great thing about New York is not the battle among the races but the time between them."

E.B. White

"In the United States there is more room where nobody is than where anybody is. That is what makes America what it is."

Gertrude Stein

"It is a great error to suppose that people are rendered stupid by remaining always in the same place."

William Cobbett

"In the spring of 1960 the Ford Foundation gave me a generous grant to tour the USA and visit the universities and institutions where strategic studies were beginning to sprout. Cynics would now say that I was being brainwashed, but if this was so it proved very effective. I already knew something about American history. I had taken the 'special subject' on the origins of the Civil War when I was at Oxford; partly because even then I realised the important part that the USA would play in the post war world, but partly also, I am afraid, because all the sources were in English. Nevertheless, I was as ignorant as were most Englishmen of my generation about the astonishing diversities and oddities that underlay the bland uniform culture with which the movies had made us familiar from birth."

Michael Howard

"I came from a very middle-class family of lawyers and architects. Travel was an immense relief – it got rid of the pressure from above and from below. If you're out on the road, people have to take you at face value."

Bruce Chatwin

"My reaction to San Francisco was that of any paid-up European; here at last was a real city, beautiful, civilised, sophisticated, innocently wicked. I felt like it was like Brighton, somewhere to spend a weekend rather than make one's home. Still after Los Angeles it was bliss."
Michael Howard

"When it is not necessary to change it is necessary not to change."
Edward Bulwer-Lytton

"Once again I was overwhelmed by that feeling I had felt so strongly on my first visit in 1946: America is still to be conquered."
François Mitterand

"The spirit of adventure makes for happy lives."
Freya Stark

"The heroic nature of train travel – its supreme confidence."
Michael Palin

"After a week and a half in Paris, with that surge of verve that always hits me when I change towns, I also changed hotels."
Elaine Dundy

"Resistance is proportional to the scale of the change one seeks to bring about. It is even the surest sign that change is on the way."
Jean Monnet

"Long shadows on County grounds – gone; warm beer going; invincible green suburbs, dog lovers, old maids bicycling to Holy Communion through morning mist – so long, farewell, goodbye."

John Major

"A little turmoil now and then, is an agreeable quickener of the sensations."

Byron

"Things do not change; we change."

Henry Thoreau

"There is no possible doubt that one thing leads to another."

Margaret Lane

"He saw his own Cornishness as the source of his strength and never tired of warning his fellow writers not to pull up their roots."

Richard Ollard on A.L. Rowse

"The answer (to achieving a fairer and more prosperous society), Kennedy sensed and then said, was to widen the terms of choice, to put into the hands of citizenry the power to achieve change through what he called 'numerous/diverse' acts of initiative and daring. Ordinary people on their own, and in their communities, could and should shape their own lives and destinies. It was not an abandonment of social conscience, but a new way to fulfil it. Robert Kennedy never used the phrase 'a third way', but that's the path he was seeking."

Anthony Sampson

"Motion is a mainspring of life."
Bruce Chatwin

"My dear, always come out of a new hole."
Noel Coward

"But above all, when local traditional farming systems disappear, communities become more and more reliant upon industrial commodity food products being transported long distances to them, with all the environmental cost (and cultural disconnection from the land) that entails. They begin to lose the traditional skills that made those places habitable in the first place, making them vulnerable in a future that may not be the same as the present. No one who works in this landscape romanticises wilderness."
James Rebanks

"It should be borne in mind that there is nothing more difficult to arrange, more doubtful of success, and more dangerous to carry through than initiating changes … The innovator makes enemies of all those who prospered under the old order, and only lukewarm support is forthcoming from those who would prosper under the new."
Niccolo Machiavelli

"I feel like a ghost wandering in a world grown alien."
Sergei Rachmaninoff

"The future is not known; it is not what older people think about but what younger people do."
Nicholas Negroponte

"Make change our friend and not our enemy."
Bill Clinton

"April is the cruellest month mixing memory and desire."
T.S. Eliot

"If I rest, I rust"
Sidney Bernstein

"And that will be England gone,
The Shadows, the meadows, the lanes,
The guildhalls, the carved choirs,
There'll be books; it will linger on
In galleries; but all that remains
For us will be concrete and tyres."
Philip Larkin

"The best travellers are illiterate, and they do not bore us with reminiscences."
Bruce Chatwin

Education, Academia and Writing

"Perhaps the most valuable result of all education is the ability to make yourself do the thing you have to do, when it ought to be done, whether you like it or not."

T.H. Huxley

"He has, thank goodness, a certain amount of original sin in him. It reveals itself in rather quiet, pleasant ways, his work has been very neat and rather good."

An Eton master

"Much of what I read was of no more lasting value than what they watch today; indeed, some of the modern television films for children are at least as good as anything I read, and are as likely to sow permanent seeds in their imagination. None the less I think that the older I grew, the more I benefited from the amount of time I spent on books. Life is short and time spent in front of the television set or computer screen is lost for ever."

Denis Healey

"A classical education is a wonderful thing. One learns from it that deep authors are not necessarily the most profound and that simplicity does not exclude profundity."
Siegmund Warburg

"In a world where change was powered by scientific knowledge, it would be sensible to include a better understanding of science among the aims of the educational system."
Jacob Bronowski

"'I love Oxford, and I hate it', he wrote in 1945. 'When I remember it I love it; for memory is a romantic organ, and perhaps I only remember my youthful illusions of the place.'"
Hugh Trevor-Roper

"Verse is memorable speech set down in metre with strict rhythms; prose is memorable speech set down without constraint of metre and in rhythms both lax and various."
Arthur Quiller-Couch

"At the same time, Trevelyan urged that the study of history gave a 'noble education' to the mind, which made it possible for men and woman to live richer, more fulfilled, more abundant lives. For great historical writing, gave 'intellectual pleasure of a very high order'. It opened up new vistas in the realm of 'personal, religious and ethical ideas.' It broadened man's horizons, stimulated his mind, and lifted his spirits. It helped him to understand great literature more fully and to enjoy art and architecture more profoundly. It enabled him to 'feel the poetry of time', to come to terms with the tragedy and the transience of the human condition, to appreciate that the past was once as real as the present, and as uncertain as the future. History, in short, inculcated a special kind of reflective wisdom about human affairs and about the human predicament: and this, combined with its more public, educative function, and the regrettable decline of the classics, made it the principal element in any contemporary humane education. A person devoid of an historical background, denied the perspective of the past on the present, incapable of understanding himself in time, was, Trevelyan, believed, 'not properly educated, either as a citizen or as an intellectual and imaginative being.'"

David Cannadine on G.M. Trevelyan

"We must respect the living, but the truth is good enough for the dead."

Voltaire

"The culture of any country cannot fail to be reflected in its system of education."

Noel Annan

"Shall I form your minds or cram you for a First?"

An Eton master

"There is a form of education which should be given to our sons, not because it is necessary, but because it benefits a free man and is noble."

Aristotle

"No, I would have hated it at Oxford. I don't want my children to go there, and I would be very upset if they did.

I've given them an apprenticeship and I've done everything I can to discourage my children from going to university. I have a fundamental disagreement with education which is based on theory as opposed to one which is constantly testing that theory in reality. So as far as my children are concerned, I would encourage them to become apprentices within the system. And when you look at the record of the business universities, they are not good. People come out with a number of ideas, and believe they are grander than they are, whereas they are less good than the people who have come up through the ranks."

James Goldsmith

"Education was free. That subject my father had written about repeatedly, as comprising his chief hope for us children, the essence of American opportunity, the treasure that no thief could touch, not even misfortune or poverty. It was the one thing he was able to promise us when he sent for us; surer, safer than bread or shelter."

Mary Antin

"Teaching is exhausting. To do it well, and Rowse could not be anything but a first-class teacher, draws on precisely those energies and responses that go into good writing. One's pupil is one's reader."

Richard Ingrams on A.L. Rowse

"The nonsense which was knocked out of them at school is all put back gently at Oxford and Cambridge."

Samuel Butler

"Teaching a subject is far and away the best way to learn it. Teaching is not confined to the classroom."

Howard Gardner

"Do you know what I'd have done if you'd got a first? Reluctantly shown you the door. I should have known you had a tired brain. This country is ruled by tired brains, and they all took firsts at the University. I will not have them in my business. A second is an excellent degree. It reveals intelligence but also a refusal to be prematurely worked out."

Lord Northcliffe

"In the information age, in which most people will be brain workers, countries without education in depth will be populated by the unemployable."

Sunday Times **leader**

"Imagination is more important than knowledge."

Albert Einstein

"It is the duty of man to be intellectually severe to himself."

G.M. Trevelyan

"A man must carry knowledge with him if he would bring knowledge home."

Dr Johnson

"To the man in the street who I'm sorry to say
Is a keen observer of life
the word 'intellectual' suggests straight away
a man who's untrue to his wife."

W.H. Auden

"Style is an ideal too, style of living, style of writing, born of disinterested thought and sweat to ennoble and preserve the thoughts and memory of an else insignificant existence."

Ralph Ellison

"Good historians are the most scarce of all writers."

A.L. Rowse

"He (Charles Henderson) was an antiquary rather than a historian. He is remembered now not for the books he wrote but for the wonderful collections of material which he bequeathed to the Royal Institution of Cornwall."

A.L. Rowse

"The point about having an open mind, like having an open mouth is to close it on something."

G.K. Chesterton

"A mathematical proof should resemble a simple and clear-cut constellation, not a scattered cluster in the Milky Way. A chess problem also has unexpectedness, and a certain economy; it is essential that the moves should be surprising, and that every piece on the board should play its part."

G.H. Hardy

"I know what I think is important for communication, and I believe communication is equal parts listening and speaking or communicating. So, it's building bridges and understanding other people's points of view, and the reasons behind things that I consider to be communication."

John Harvey-Jones

"Eggheads of the world unite; you have nothing to lose but your yokes."

Adlai Stevenson

"Of all the pursuits ever invented by man for separating the faculty of argument from the capacity of belief, the art of debating is the most effective."

Walter Bagehot

"From the inability to let well alone; from too much zeal for the new and contempt for the old; from putting knowledge before wisdom, science before art, and cleverness before common sense; from treating patients as cases, and from making the cure of the disease more grievous than its endurance, Good Lord deliver us."

Sir Robert Hutchison

They are "something wider and more intrinsic to the human beings who hold them than opinions or even principles ... (they) are the central complex of relations of a man towards himself and to the external world."

Isaiah Berlin on the subject of values

"Intuition, I have always believed, is really reasoning speeded up."

Elaine Dundy

"When my first novel was published, my father got together all the elders of my tribe to buy me a pen. Well, this will buy me a lot of pens. I dedicate this prize to all those who suffer in public and in private, and who never give up dreaming."

Ben Oki, on receiving the Booker Prize for *The Famished Road*

"Though his response to books is personal, it never becomes capricious or arbitrary. He never falls into the error of smaller men who say, 'I like that', 'I disliked that, I may be wrong, but that's how I feel,' and think they are being frank. So they are, but they are discrediting frankness and making it flimsy and unacceptable. Their confessions of faith contract one's heart. Dr Trevelyan's expand it, for he can amplify and illustrate."

E.M. Forster

"I have no room for new ideas."

Jonathan Swift

"Let no one say that I have said nothing new; the arrangement of the material is new."

Blaise Pascal

"Adjectives are Sirens; they betray all whom their music beguiles. Enslave them. And you are master of the poetic art."

George Rylands

"The town, not the country, was 'the true scene for a man of letters.'"

A.J. Ayer

"A man always looks dead after his life has appeared."

Byron

"Why gaze into the crystal when you can read the book."

Aneurin Bevan

"Say what you have to say in the fewest possible words."
Aristotle

"No whiches, thats and whos."
Bruce Chatwin

"People say life is the thing, but I prefer reading."
Logan Pearsall Smith

"The word once uttered returns not."
Horace

"In the beginning was the Word."
The Bible

"Persuasion is the only true intellectual process."
Matthew Arnold

"What I consider the richest cake which is baked in the oven of the gods: the ecstasy and the exasperation of the art of writing."
Hugh Trevor-Roper

"Read no History, nothing but biography."
Disraeli

"Those of us who presume to write books would appear to fall into two categories: the ones who 'dig in' and the ones who move. There are writers who can only function 'at home', with the right chair, the shelves of dictionaries and encyclopaedias, and now perhaps the word processor. And there are

those, like myself, who are paralysed by home, for whom home is synonymous with the proverbial writer's block, and who believe naively that all would be well if only they were somewhere else."
Bruce Chatwin

"There is a great deal of nonsense talked about writing novels. The common assumption is that it is easy; we all have a novel within us, so they say. People talk carelessly about their intention to 'write it all down one day'. They encourage others with the same recklessness. As if it were the simplest thing in the world. It is a job to write a novel."
Jennie Erdal

"He was a highly visual writer. Writing is the painting of the voice," he wrote in his notebook. "The more it resembles it, the better it is."
Bruce Chatwin

"Words and phrases are the only thing that matters." "There is one thing that matters – to set a chime of words tinkling or twinkling in the minds of a few fastidious people."
Logan Pearsall Smith

"Cooke was comfortable in his study, which had grown around him like a second skin. In a rare act of self-revelation, he had allowed the *Observer* newspaper (in 1986) to look around the place for the regular feature 'A Room of my Own'. And even more rarely, he was delighted with the result. The interviewer, Ena Kendall, was enthralled from the moment she was invited to step along the central corridor with 'its delicate Hepplewhite furniture and thick pale Indian carpet' and intrigued by what she saw along the way; 'Open doors allowed glimpses of splendid rooms, the walls hung with paintings. And then, to the study, which – Cooke told her – had seen some two hundred reporters pass through its portals, almost all of whom referred to it afterwards as his 'red study' or his 'book lined' room. It was both of these things, of course, but he found the repetition tiresome. 'Once, in a spasm of mischief,' he confessed to her, he had removed every picture that was not a nude in the hope that an interviewer from the *New Yorker* would refer to a 'nude lined' study – to no avail."

Nick Clarke on Alistair Cooke

"You don't know what will happen until you start writing. Only then do you discover things that previously you knew nothing about. There is a level at which you know what you are doing, it is a conscious process; you decide what to put in this chapter, what to leave for the next. But at another level, there seem to be deep forces at work that take you in unexpected directions. How much does the unconscious influence writing? And in some sense, it does seem reasonable to regard a novel as an accident of the unconscious, not in the sense of mishap, but in the sense of various strands colliding."

Jennie Erdal

"Dear Captain … I'm delighted to hear you begin to see the nucleus of a library – it is one of the great pleasures, and I find I no longer deride people who do little else but collect books. I hope to have some more for you soon."

Alistair Cooke to his son, nicknamed 'Captain'

"I don't do much writing in my room. For that, I need other conditions and other places. But I can think there, listen to music, read in bed, and take notes. It is, when all is said, a place to hang one's hat."

Bruce Chatwin

"Perhaps this is why I carried on working years after it would have become possible to live by my writing – if occasionally, precariously. I found to be part of the working world was a powerful inspiration as well as providing useful background information."

P.D. James

"This I learnt from him and believed, and I still believe it, and shall, I hope, continue, like Gibbon, to value reading above the wealth of India. For in his life and conversation, among the tinkle of coronets and the wild extravagant gossip, and the exquisite relish of high life and la comédie humaine, of which he was also witness, he illustrated this philosophy to me so vividly that if it has not become mine, at least mine can never be altogether emancipated from its influence."

Hugh Trevor-Roper on Logan Pearsall Smith

"He told a graduate student that he wrote everything four or five times over before he would let it go to print. The impression of effortlessness required painstaking endeavour. Many of his letters mentioned the difficulties he was encountering with the form of the book. The essential problem seems to have been one of incorporating analysis of the social structure within a narrative framework."

Jonathan Sperber on Karl Marx

"Whenever I have been in residence, the place becomes a sea of books and papers and unmade beds and clothes thrown this way and that. But the Tower is a place where I have always worked, clearheadedly and well, in winter and summer, by day or night - and the places you work well are the places you love the most."

Bruce Chatwin

"Anatole France described his literary criticism as 'the adventures of my soul among masterpieces.'"

Michael Henderson

"Dreams and recollection are here (at All Souls) more real than reality. It is this quality of his consciousness that gives Rowse's history and poetry their peculiar power. When reality in the ordinary sense forces itself upon him the vision fades. 'The letter killeth but the spirit giveth life.'"

Philip Larkin.

"Words are the ammunition of the advocate; simple but telling words placed in the right order. It is remarkable how powerful words can be. A love of literature and an appreciation of the written word, that which Norman Birkett refers to 'as the well-stocked mind', make a good background for an advocate. As an advocate I always wished that I had been better read."

Thomas Grant quoting Jeremy Hutchinson

"There are two reasons why I offered the Morgan Library a choice of my books. One is that, in spite of the size of the library, it does not feel like an institution. The books seem to be loved and cared for as they are in a private library."

Robert B. Silvers

"One of the large French rivers – wide, placid, seemingly endless, no current, occasional felicities on the bank, shallow and just moving."

George Moore on the writing style of Henry James

"This then is style. As technically manifested in Literature it is the power to touch with ease, grace, precision, any note in the gamut of human thought or emotion. But essentially it resembles good manners. It comes of endeavouring to understand others, of thinking of them rather than of yourself – of thinking, that is, with the heart as well as the head. It gives rather than receives; it is nobly careless of thanks or applause, not being fed by these but rather sustained and continually refreshed by an inward loyalty to the best. Yes, like 'character' it has its altar within; to that retires for counsel, from that fetches its illumination, to ray outwards. Cultivate, Gentlemen, that habit of withdrawing to be advised by the best. So, says Fenelon, 'you will find yourself infinitely quieter, your words will be fewer and more effectual; and while you make less ado, what you do will be more profitable.'"

Arthur Quiller-Couch

"It is a remarkable write, but not an irresistible read."

Unattributed

"They are agreeable enough but if they'd been books, I shouldn't have read them."

Goethe on the Schlegel brothers

"True knowledge is sedentary."

François Mitterand

"Books do furnish a room, and the best books decorate a life."
Michael Henderson

"By the complexity of its wax cells the bee puts more than one architect to shame. But from the outset, what differentiates the worst architect from the most expert bee is that he has built the cell in his head before building it in the hive."
Karl Marx

"We also need to understand something of the culture of other peoples; here the poets and novelists can teach us more than the so-called political scientists."
Denis Healey

"A great memory does not make a philosopher; any more than a dictionary can be called a grammar."
Cardinal Newman

"Knowledge is power."
Francis Bacon

"Everybody gets so much information all day long that they lose their common sense."
Gertrude Stein

"Do you think that love is the greatest emotion? Why do you know a greater one? Yes. Interest."
Thomas Mann

"You can never dispense with thinking."
Matthew Parris

"Pampering the mind is just as important as pampering the body. Literature is a utopia for the soul and the habit of reading a refuge from life's difficulties. Read to remember or read to forget, you are not alone, but part of a broader republic of letters, a secret society, that exalts in the sweet serenity of books."

Ross Gay

"Teaching experiences are simply the formal organised part of a lifetime of teaching and learning under many circumstances and in many places. The student body at Chicago was of consistently high quality, and it did not hesitate to make it clear if you failed to explain something to their satisfaction. I learned as much from them as they did from me."

Milton Friedman

"These scrolls were part of the Library of Qumran, copies of the Bible and commentaries, but recognisably arising from the same impulse as the one that created the Bodleian: the desire to cling to our culture, which has made us what we are."

Alberto Manguel

"Around 350 BC, Aristotle defined human beings as – 'the rational animal' or, more accurately the animal that has language. Language, above all, is what distinguishes us from other creatures on the planet. The development of language freed us from the world of physical objects and substituted a world of symbols. The lower animals may also communicate with one another in a primitive way and may even be taught the meaning of a few of our human symbols – a dog can learn to understand 'sit' or 'come' for example. But for perhaps forty thousand years only humans were 'zoon logon echon' (the rational animal): the animal with language."

Robert Harris.

"A mathematician, like a painter or a poet, is a maker of patterns."

G.H. Hardy

"Proper words in proper places, make the true definition of a style."

Jonathan Swift

"Do right and don't write."

Alistair Cooke

"Vulgarity is not, as George Eliot would have it, something to be avoided at all costs. And you should not, in life or in literature, be afraid of sentimentality either. Some of the best things in life, works that are a pleasure to be handed on to the generations to come, have vulgarity and sentimentality in spades."

John Mortimer

"Southerners too often forget that from the eighteenth century onwards intellectual life in the British provinces was often as stimulating as London."

Denis Healey

"Intelligence, highly awakened, is intuition which is the only true guide in life."

Jonathan Swift

"What does realism as a literary mode do? It operates through absolute attention to the appearance of things."

John Carey

"A mother whale's advice to her young: 'Beware, my dears, it is when you are spouting that you are most likely to be harpooned.' A useful opening to a speech when excusing its brevity."

David B. McCulloch

"Baldwin's contribution was a bit of a ramble, but his earnest tone of voice drew you into what he was saying. I do not think I ever heard him utter a cliché."

Bill Deedes on Stanley Baldwin

"You learn to speak in public exactly as you learn to ride a bicycle: you keep falling off."

Bernard Shaw

"Of all the talents bestowed upon men, none is more precious as the gift of oratory … Abandoned by his party, betrayed by his friends, stripped of his offices, whoever can command this power is still formidable."

Winston Churchill

"To fight with form, to wrestle and to rage
Till at the last upon the conquered page
The shadows of created beauty fall."

Alfred Douglas

Money, Business and Leadership

"Just for a handful of silver he left us,
Just for a riband to stick in his coat."
Robert Browning

"We may see the small value God has for riches by the people he gives them to."
Alexander Pope

"If you want to make money, go where the money is."
Joe Kennedy

"Greed has been severely underestimated and denigrated – unfairly so in my opinion. I mean there is nothing wrong with avarice as a motive, as long as it doesn't lead to dishonest or anti-social conduct. I don't think greed, as such, is anything to be proud of, but a spirit of moderate acquisitiveness is not un-akin to self-preservation. It is a motive that has not failed to move me from time to time."
Conrad Black

"The older I am the more I feel possessions are a burden more than an asset. To make one's life simple is for me a supreme urge."

Siegmund Warburg

"But I hated to waste my time contending for money. I had no taste for trade, and I still haven't."

François Mitterand

"On the one hand I noted how stupefying and tyrannous a god Mammon is and into what a conformity he can drill his votaries, until they die of stomach ulcers or alcoholism."

Maurice Bowra

"Reading it, I found myself increasingly unable to answer a simple question about life in this country: why are we less human and less kind when prosperous than we managed to be when we were poor? No washing machines, no Starbucks, no computers, no television – but people evidently knew how to listen in a spirit of fairness."

David Kynaston

"The pursuit of wealth is, to the mass of mankind, the great source of moral improvement. I really should on every account be sorry, Gentlemen, to exaggerate, but indeed one is taken by surprise, one is startled, on meeting with so very categorical a contradiction of our Lord, St Paul, St Chrysostom, St Leo, and all Saints."

Cardinal Newman

"Nobody would remember the Good Samaritan if he'd only had good intentions; he had money as well."
Margaret Thatcher

"In all investment matters the will to pay is often as important as the ability to pay."
Lewis Whyte

"Money which should be the servant of those who possess it can become a tyrant if it is taken as an emblem of social status."
Siegmund Warburg

"The art of investment banking consists of taking a button and making a suit out of it."
André Meyer

"A tangled network of mantraps for conscience."
William Gladstone on income tax

"At the back of every great fortune lies a great crime."
Honore de Balzac

"It was from Marx that he learned, and continued to believe, that at the base of human history lay its economic facts."
Richard Ollard on A.L. Rowse

"Sentimentality and nostalgia (derived from hymn singing) may be – even though shallow and fleeting – an apprehension of what I referred to earlier as that mystery which we call the numinous (mystery of spirituality) that may lead boys, to associate with the Chapel some alternative to that self-centred materialism which is the besetting evil of our affluent society."

Donald Hughes, Headmaster, Rydal School

"The horse does all the work, and the coachman gets the tip."

Joe Eaton

"Money has never been my God, I've never bothered about it. I had to do something for myself. I felt that if I wasn't to get on people would not respect me. I would just be one of the masses."

Jack Cohen

"Charity saves from death."

Old Jewish Proverb

"No one ever went broke underestimating the taste of the American Public."

H.L. Mencken

"The American ebullience came from a belief that individual enterprise and energy, encouraged by state and local government, could bring an unprecedented level of well-being for all the people."

Daniel Boorstin

"In this matter I have been led astray by the temptation of money. Security is desirable, but not above all things."

A.L. Rowse

"I have to be ruled by pragmatism. My *raison d'être* is to satisfy the customer, and decisions have to be made to create maximum wealth. I must use logic to suppress my ego, otherwise it is impossible to be objective. I do not allow conversation to take place when we have to decide, all data must be collected, and the logical decision will be taken."
Arnold Weinstock

"The excessive analysis of a situation can easily lead to paralysis."
Siegmund Warburg

"Britain has a system in which the top salaries are paid in finance, and there are cosy, high income cartels protecting those who can pass stiff examinations for the professions. Result: the City gets the pick of the most enterprising; the professions get those who are high in brainpower but averse to risk – and industry and commerce are left, all too often, to those who are neither particularly enterprising nor particularly clever.
Anthony Harris

"Negotiation being first cousin to flirtation."
J.P. Morgan

"Essentially Clore had more innate respect for human failings than for human strengths. In the realms of business, he regarded weakness as the main driving force and as a profound sceptic he exploited to the full this cynical and melancholic view of life. He expected the worst of people and was rarely surprised. In probing for weakness, he sought to undermine the other person's confidence and in so doing he obtained an abundance of gratuitous information and facts, much of it meaningful. He sifted the salient bits and without hesitation acted upon what he had garnered."

Charles Gordon on Charles Clore

"The only ideas which interested them were those which they had in common and repeated like incantations to one another in the hope that this would make them feel good."

Maurice Bowra

"I must regard everything we don't do well as a personal failure … I am exposed to the world and to my own work people, and this is a constant and considerable pressure. Public confidence is the key to the success and impetus of any firm. If I don't do well then people lose confidence. I am responsible for everything. I can't shift the blame if we have a bad manager, it's my fault for putting him there."

Arnold Weinstock

"An open-ended financial situation was diametrically opposed to his lifelong habit, indeed his fear, of going out of his depth."

Charles Gordon on Charles Clore

"The inescapable truth is that the problems of the future are sown in the acts of today."

Victoria Glendinning

"I liked the optimism they brought to everything they did, the informality, the sense that anything was possible. They were a breath of fresh air, really bold, no challenge too big and the atmosphere they helped to create was great for people like me."

Charles Dunstone on Richard Branson and Tony Blair

"Equality of opportunity means equal opportunity to be unequal."

Iain Macleod

"The capacity to detect wants and the alertness to mobilize labour and capital to satisfy them."

Israel Kirzner on the attributes of the entrepreneur

"Every entrepreneur is a high wire specialist."

William H. Draper III

"I do not believe that entrepreneurs should spend too much time thinking about what has happened in the past – either successes or failures – except as experience to draw upon for the future"

Arturo Ferruzzi

"It was a politics shaped to a 'boom and bust' economy in which the national dream was to make a fortune – or if a depression and calamity came, to wipe out one's losses through easy bankruptcy laws so that with an economic upturn one could start over again. The role of government was to aid these entrepreneurs, whatever their local or regional interests and to place no impediment in their way."

David Boorstin

"Short agreements make long friends."
Robert Louis Stevenson

"Be kind to people on the way up because you will meet them again on your way down."
Wilson Mizner

"You do have to listen a lot, but you can't be so democratic as to listen to everyone. Part of what a brand offers is a specific point of view."
Christopher Bailey

"The doctor who makes a friend of his patients, the lawyer who defends death penalty cases in distant countries for no fee, the schoolteacher who opens a child's eyes to a new world of books and poetry – such people do nothing that can be measured in marketplaces."
John Mortimer

"The Cotton-Clore business environment was where I also discovered that an entrepreneur's strength of will was more vital to his survival than his talent for money making."
Charles Gordon

"A bribe is a bet."
Aristotle Onassis

"When it comes to loving and understanding borrowing clients, however, the Japanese have the more appropriate tradition. Like the German banks, they have deep, committed and supportive relationships with their major clients. This is the kind of banking which the Bank of England has long sought to encourage, with very little effect. It might now be about to discover that throwing the City to the sharks is more educative than any number of cups of tea in Threadneedle Street."

Anthony Harris

"The change became complete in the Thatcher years. As the factory gates closed there were no jobs for manufacturers anymore and we became a nation of shopkeepers and hairdressers. It was then that politicians, 'entrepreneurs', and practically everyone else began to speak, in tones of religious awe about the 'marketplace'. Ignore the fact that Jesus made some un-called for remarks about the poor being blessed, forget the sometimes uncommercial nature of art or literature that reveals the truth about our lives, and instead take everything down to the marketplace to discover how well it tells us how much it is worth."

John Mortimer

"Economies grew with innovation, risk taking, credit, and strong public and private leadership."

Richard Parker

"The main support of life is work – if it doesn't let you down."

Albert Camus

"The entrepreneur needs the kind of education that prepared him for surviving in the "open". He has to learn to build a structure of relationships outside the established organisations."

Stephen Aris

"Management is the arrangement of the most economical use of resources."

Arnold Weinstock

"He did not build a business but made an existing one (GEC) more profitable and efficient by a programme of ruthless rationalisation and simplification."

Unattributed on Arnold Weinstock

"To undertake new things is difficult and constitutes a distinct economic function, first because they lie outside of the routine tasks which everybody understands and, secondly, because the environment resists in many ways that vary, according to social conditions, from simple refusal either to finance or buy a new thing, to physical attack on the man who tries to produce it. To act with confidence beyond the range of familiar beacons and overcome that resistance requires aptitudes that are present in only a small fraction of the population and that define the entrepreneurial type as well as the entrepreneurial function. This function does not essentially consist in either inventing anything or otherwise creating the conditions which the enterprise exploits. It consists of getting things done."

Joseph Schumpeter

"Clore was an alchemist who with concentrated ruthlessness and immense sense of character made a colossal fortune out of nothing."

Charles Gordon on Charles Clore

"Meyer considered himself first and foremost an investment banker. The main business of Lazard, as far as he was concerned, was advice to corporations: on acquisitions and mergers and divestitures, and above all on financing. He called it 'Financial Engineering'."

John Chernow on Andre Meyer

"I have long believed that a feeling for economics is something people are born with rather than acquire through education. Many highly intelligent and even highly trained professional economists know the words but don't get the music. On the other hand, people with little or no training in economics may have an intuitive feeling for it."

Niall Ferguson

"We scarcely ever heard the word 'entrepreneur' and if we did it was used to describe the middleman who produced nothing."

John Mortimer

"This was a business milieu where being indecisive or hesitant or weak could quite literally be fatal. It was also a business milieu where I first learnt that in almost every case the leading characters were prompted not by greed, nor by a lust for power, but were motivated by a profound psychological and social need for acceptance. I found to my surprise that, pervading every relationship, there was a peculiar aroma of insecurity. An entrepreneur's sudden course of action was almost never inspired by logic but almost always by an emotion brought to the surface erupting from a feeling of anxiety, from a sense of insecurity, from a desire 'to show them' – them being a member of the establishment, or a partner or a competitor or a family relation. If there is one common trait in every entrepreneur, it is that he is a thoroughly insecure animal whose main drive is vanity and whose main passion is a worship of prestige. His need for money is a need for protection."

Charles Gordon

"He has arguably done more than anyone else to promote free market economics and the broader ideology surrounding it. By mainstreaming libertarianism, he helped to change the way people think. Absent his money and strategic vision, the country (USA) would be a different place. Few people can claim they changed the world, but this is undeniably true of Charles. And he's not done yet."

Daniel Schulman on Charles Koch

"In 1940 the issue was clear, and the victory was primarily and fundamentally a moral victory long before it could become a material victory. I do not believe that I am alone in asking whether the time has not come for the same solution. The question is again a moral one and a moral triumph is the first condition of economic success."

Donald Hughes, Headmaster, Rydal School

"Why did the economic and social intellectual life of the Roman Catholic countries sink or stagnate, while that of the Protestant countries bounded forward, in the three centuries after the Reformation?" Hugh acknowledges the significance of religious differences in the emergence of a capitalist economy. He concluded that the Protestant countries were or became more forward-looking than their Catholic counterparts. He argued that the Roman Catholic Church, in its medieval form, had been compatible with capitalist expansion. "The counter-reformation might be seen as a great spiritual revival; but sociologically it represented an enormous strengthening in the bureaucratic structure of society, a huge increase in the tax burden and in the controls the church imposed on economic activity. Artisans as well as entrepreneurs fled to the less restrictive, more tolerant countries of the Protestant north."

Max Weber on Hugh Trevor-Roper

"The most dangerous thing that could happen to the bank (admittance to orthodox circles) as it would lead to a propensity for laziness and complacency."

Siegmund Warburg

"Sound ideas don't die – they survive to meet a good moment."

Victoria Glendinning

"Certainly, this force of destiny relates to human leadership, and gives leaders a special charisma. It relates to creativity. It is a quasi-paranormal experience which can be part of a higher mystical experience, as it was with Socrates, St Gregory the Thaumaturge, or Henry Moore himself. It can however be terribly destructive. Hitler seems to have had a psychological experience similar to that of Joan of Arc; in his case it led to the Holocaust; in her case to the independence of France."

John O'Donohue

"The role of a leader is to be a self-starter who inspires others. Teamwork is important but there has to be a leader."

John Spedan Lewis

"Any truly valuable experience which leads an individual to modify his approach to managing or to life in general, may be untidy, indistinct and even painful."
Arnold Weinstock

"I could go further and say that for management to be good it generally must be experienced."
Roy Thomson

"The great leader knows that most success comes from making a few large decisions correctly rather than trying to be involved in making lots of small choices. He will understand that there are others in the organisation capable of doing things that he himself cannot do or not do as well. He will derive more satisfaction from the achievements of his organisation than from his own accomplishment, will not demand outlandish compensation for himself, will treat the organisations money as if it were his own with no need to be singled out by the spotlight. He will probably watch and listen more than he talks. Will not radiate anxiety when the chips are down, will have a keen understanding of what he doesn't know and a fetching sense of humility. If he does his job well, people will see him as being tough but fair rather than capricious and mercurial. He will definitely not feel the need to be universally loved. At the end of his tenure, knowing that his time has ended, he will relinquish authority with grace and will not sour the life of his successor. Compare this with the capable Manager who has attained his position by attrition, by being politically acceptable or by being a faithful, long-suffering servant. He would concentrate on making sure nothing goes wrong on his watch, will be wary of offending others, will shy away from making difficult decisions, will be at ease with the imperfections of compromise, will allow his strategy to be dictated by others, will find refuge in appeasement and court the affection of those around him. When he retires the organisation will be little different from the one he inherited. It will definitely not have achieved anything remarkable. The great leader has two other traits that separate him from other helmsmen. The first is obsession. Obsessives, those who cannot imagine doing anything else with their lives find their work more fulfilling than those who find themselves in a profession because it was expected of them. The second trait of the distinctive leader is his capacity for dealing with people. Those leaders will be able to extract extraordinary levels of performance and commitment from their colleagues and employees."

Alice Schroeder, recounting Warren Buffett's view on leadership

"Social position is nothing to me, and never has been anything. Titles don't appeal to me … You are a young man. Don't worry about these things. The important thing is poise. How a man handles a situation is a much more important thing than the situation itself. Poise in all things and at all times."

Paul C Cabot

"The more one is exposed to the necessity of making decisions, the better one's decision making becomes."

John C. Bogle

"Getting results through people is a skill that cannot be learned in the classroom."

John Paul Getty

"One of the qualities of a good manager is to take as little account as possible of the mediocre – when mediocre people have influence, they exercise it in the wrong direction."

Siegmund Warburg

"Leadership of any sort makes for a certain kind of solitariness … Any individual will have only so much energy and personal resources, and (in my case) they have been spread very widely. So, one is inclined to do what one has to do and be where one has to be. The rest of the time, as far as I am concerned, I tend to pull up the drawbridge in order that I can refuel the boilers. There are times when I need to get right away from the conflab of meeting the public or whatever."

Sara Morrison

"If you don't have fun in your work, you can never give your best."

Geoffrey Ellis

"If it rested ultimately with Sidney, it was because it was his enthusiasm and nerve that had to carry the day and because that had always been his role in Granada; the man who had ideas and took decisions while others deliberated, reasoned with him, voiced their fears and doubts and in the end interpreted what had been decided to the outside world."

Caroline Moorehead on Sidney Bernstein

"I cannot imagine how anyone without firm conviction and deep inner beliefs can be an effective leader."

Alex Ferguson

History, Politics and War

"Quinquireme of Nineveh from distant Ophir
Rowing home to haven in sunny Palestine,
With a cargo ivory,
And apes and peacocks,
Sandalwood, cedarwood, and sweet white wine.
Stately Spanish galleon coming from the Isthmus,
Dipping through the Tropics by the palm-green shores,
With a cargo of diamonds,
Emeralds, amethysts,
Topazes, and cinnamon, and gold moidores.
Dirty British Coaster with a salt-caked smoke stack
Butting through the channel in the mad March days,
With a cargo of Tyne coal,
Road-rails, pig-lead,
Firewood, iron-ware, and cheap tin trays."
John Masefield

"The whole history of the world is summed up in the fact that, when nations are strong, they are not always just, and when they wish to be just, they are often no longer strong."
Winston Churchill

"Very deep in the well of the past. Should we not call it bottomless."

Thomas Mann

"Metahistory attempts to analyse the profound spiritual and factual forces at play. From this analysis, it tried to make an intelligent surmise about the future. When this method is well employed (as it was by de Tocqueville or Nietzsche) the results can be almost clairvoyant."

Michael White

"The white man will be taking his leave of the hummingbird and the stag and will see the end of that which was life. After that, all that will remain to him is to survive. Paradoxically perhaps, it is the very sense of a general and universal awareness that makes the statement so accurate. Seattle's (an American Chief of the Duwamish tribe in a letter to the President of the United States) approach to the world was cosmological: contemporary forecasters are materialistic. Therein lies the difference between history and metahistory.

If metahistorical forces did not exist, history would follow a regulated course and there would be neither wars nor revolutions. Indeed, the reason economists and futurologists have had such a dismal record is that they extrapolate from the present and assume that this trend will continue in the future. In simple terms this is like someone driving an automobile while looking out of the rear-view mirror and being surprised when the car runs off the road."

William Irwin Thompson

"I don't mean to sound didactic, and of course in a way we had done it all through our history. But in the cold war, when our enemies lied, they lied to conceal the wretchedness of their system. Whereas when we lied, we concealed our virtues. Even from ourselves. We concealed the very things that made us right. Our respect for the individual, our love of variety and argument, our belief that you can only govern fairly with the consent of the governed, our capacity to see the other fellow's view – most notably in the countries we exploited, almost to death, for our own ends. In our supposed ideological rectitude, we sacrificed our compassion to the great god of indifference. We protected the strong against the weak, and we perfected the art of the public lie. We made enemies of decent reformers and friends of the most disgusting potentates. And we scarcely paused to ask ourselves how much longer we could defend our society by these means and remain a society worth defending."

John Le Carré

"History, in short, inculcated a special kind of reflective wisdom about human affairs and about the human predicament; and this combined with its more public, educative function, and the regrettable decline of the classics, made it the principal element in any contemporary humane education. A person devoid of an historical background, denied the perspective of the past on the present, incapable of understanding himself in time, was, Trevelyan believed, 'not properly educated', either as a citizen or as an intellectual and imaginative being."

David Cannadine

"In an age when the structure of English Society is being eroded from the roots, the church needs clergy, and society needs writers who have a sense of, and a feeling for, history."
Terry Waite

"The trace of memory, Bragg shows us, is an enduring inheritance for each and every one of us."
Book critic on Melvyn Bragg's *A Son of War*

"Similarly, I learned that it is not possible to understand politics, particularly in a world which is changing as fast as ours after the end of the Cold War, without knowing something of history."
Denis Healey

"Living history was not like reading it. History, once written, has the illusion of inevitability, and nowhere is this probably more true that in the histories we have of the short-lived Second Republic."
George Dallas

"What I really believe is that those with curiosity, whatever their educational and occupational backgrounds, are bound to have interest in and acquire some knowledge about the past; and that those without it are likely to be dull men and uncomprehending rulers."
Roy Jenkins

"Anachronism and provincialism are two of the deadly sins of history, both equally due to a sheer ignorance of what things are like elsewhere, which even limitless reading and the power of imagination can only rarely overcome."

Eric Hobsbawm

"Jack's concerns with his situation may have owed something to his dawning realisation that the P.T. boats, however glamorous in the popular imagination, were of questionable military utility. Fast, nimble and versatile, their prows riding high in the water, the boats could make hit-and-run attacks in narrow waters or close to land and they were excellent for rescuing downed fliers and trapped Marines. But their torpedoes, designed in the 1920's were outmoded, the guns were inadequate, and the radios frequently conked out. Worst of all with their thin mahogany shells (two layers of one inch planking) and heavy fuel loads the TT boats were, to say the least, combustible, prone to turning into floating infernos when hit. Kennedy was drilled on the importance of avoiding detection by enemy aircraft and ships, which meant, above all, operating under the cloak of darkness and moving stealthily. It took guts to make your close approach in this way – the enemy could obliterate you in an instant if its lookouts ever saw you. "The glamour of the PT's just isn't except to the outsider" he wrote "it's just a matter of night after night patrols at low speed in rough water – two hours on - then sailing out and going on again for another two hours". "As a matter of fact, this job is somewhat like sailing, in that we spend most of our time trying to get the boat running faster." James Michener offered in Tales of the South Pacific: "They shook the stomach's out of many men who rode them. They had no defensive armour. In many instances they were suicide boats."

Frederik Logewall

"There is no inevitability in history except as men make it."
Felix Frankfurter

"History is unkind to its losers."
George Dallas

"I am convinced that the most congenial, as well as the most concrete and practical, approach to history is the biographical, through the lives of the great men whose actions have been so much part of history, and those careers in turn have been so moulded and formed by events."
A.L. Rowse

"A society unaware of its history is like a person suffering from amnesia. It cannot function efficiently."
Norman Davies

"Blindness to the past is a precursor of future folly."
***The Times* Leader**

"History, at least in its state of ideal perfection, is a compound of poetry and philosophy. It impresses general truths on the mind by a vivid representation of particular character and incidents."
Lord Macaulay

"I think it was Utz who just convinced me that history is always our guide for the future, and always full of capricious surprises. The future itself is a dead land because it does not yet exist."
Bruce Chatwin

"The longer you look back, the further you can look forward."
Winston Churchill

"History is the only guide we have for understanding what is happening today. We are only just discovering that much which is at first sight difficult to understand in Eastern Europe or the former Soviet Union becomes all too intelligible if we read something of the history of those regimes over the last thousand years. And it remains terribly true that those who do not learn from history are condemned to repeat it."
Denis Healey

"History helps to lengthen perspective and by so doing discourages excessive partisanship. This must, however, be qualified by saying that it applies to a reasonably detached view of history and not to living in its shadow with an obsessive concentration. No communities are more difficult to bring together – Northern Ireland, Cyprus – than those where the contemplation of ancient wrongs is a way of life."
Roy Jenkins

"The appeal of history to us all is in the last analysis poetic. But the poetry of history does not consist of imagination roaming at large, but of imagination pursuing the fact and fastening upon it. That which compels the historian to 'scorn delights and live laborious days' is the ardour of his own curiosity to know what really happened long ago in that land of mystery which we call the past. To peer into that magic mirror and see fresh figures there every day is a burning desire that consumes and satisfies him all his life, that carries him each morning, eager as a lover, to the library. The dead were and are not. Their place knows them no more and is ours today. Yet they were once as real as we, and we shall tomorrow be shadows like them."

G.M. Trevelyan

"History is everywhere. It seeps into the soil, the sub-soil. Like rain, or hail, or snow, or blood. A house remembers. An outhouse remembers. A people ruminate. The tale differs with the teller."

Edna O'Brien

"The twentieth century, I find, is a fascinating century to live in and to study – when, since the 5th century, was Europe so interesting and mutable to observe?"

Hugh Trevor-Roper

"See how bored we have grown of ourselves in the modern Western world and how people can fight back and shape their futures using their history as an advantage, not an obligation. All of this has made me believe more strongly, not less, in our farming way of life and why it matters in the Lake District."

James Rebanks

"The history of the world is but the history of great men."

Thomas Carlyle

"Legal history for him was not simply the jumble of technical facts that he had been taught, or a form of social history obscured by lawyer's jargon, but 'the intellectual history of society.'"

S.F.C. Milson

"Adversity and affliction beset our world. This book has been written in the belief that the problems surrounding us are of our own making, and that our failure to deal with them is unnecessary. Our afflictions are the legacy of short-sightedness and ignorance, not mankind's innate inability to right his own wrongs."

Michael White

"It is European techniques, European examples, European ideas which have shaken the non-European world out of its past – out of barbarism in Africa, out of a far older, slower, more majestic civilisation in Asia; and the history of the world for the last five centuries, in so far as it has significance, has been European History."

Hugh Trevor-Roper

"Those who cannot remember the past are condemned to repeat it."

Santayana

"History is a set of lies everyone agrees on."

Napoleon

"It takes a great deal of history to produce a little literature."

Henry James

"To be ignorant of what occurred before you were born is to remain a child forever."

Cicero

"If a free society cannot help the many who are poor, it cannot save the few who are rich."

John F. Kennedy

"A Soviet joke:
Q – What's the difference between Capitalism and Communism?
A – Under capitalism. Man exploits man. Under communism it is exactly the opposite."

David Levy

"Our problem is not that we are being Americanised. In spite of the massive impact of cultural and economic Americanisation, the rest of the world, even the capitalist world, has so far been strikingly resistant to following the model of U.S. politics and society. This is probably because America is less of a coherent and therefore exportable social and political model of a capitalist liberal democracy, based on the universal principles of universal freedom, than its patriotic ideology and constitution suggests. So, far from being a clear example which the rest of the world can imitate, the USA, however powerful and influential, remains an unending process, distorted by big money and public emotion, of tinkering with institutions, public and private, to make them fit realities unforeseen in the unalterable text of a 1787 constitution. It simply does not lend itself to copying."

Eric Hobsbawm

"A bowl of bitter tears."

James Joyce describes the Atlantic Ocean

"Today all peoples for better or worse, aspire to Americanisation."

A.L. Rowse

"He employed the language of empathy, emphasising America's shared dreams and shared destiny as a people."

Fredrick Logevall on JFK

"Still the greatest and most honourable adventure."

John Buchan

"Once you get a doctrine, that is the end of you. Pragmatic politics are the only good ones."

Harold Macmillan

"Europe must either push itself to the fore in the cybernetic race or see itself die."

Michael White

"A scrupulous man is impractical in politics."

Anthony Trollope

"The discussion ranged over war, peace – and the business of politics. Cooke said that he had never contemplated the life of a politician, because 'I was brought up to believe that there is always much to be said on both sides', and in any matter of serious import, there might be three, four or five sides to be taken into account."

John Le Carré

"Our problem is rather that the U.S. empire does not know what it wants to do or can do with its power, or its limits. It merely insists that those who are not with it are against it. That is the problem of living at the apex of the 'American Century'."

Eric Hobsbawm

"Imagine if at this moment, instead of the Queen, we had a gentleman in evening clothes, ill-made, probably from Moss Bros, with a white tie, going about everywhere, who had been elected by some deal made between the extreme Right and the extreme Left …! Then we would all wait for the next one, another little man, who is it going to be? … 'Give it to "X", you know he's been such a bad Chancellor of the Exchequer, instead of getting rid of him, let's make him the next President …' Can you imagine it? I mean, it doesn't make sense, that would be the final destruction of colour and life and the sense of the past in this country, wouldn't it?"

Harold Macmillan

"The kingly office is entitled to no respect. It was originally procured by highwayman's methods; it remains a perpetuated crime, can never be anything but the symbol of a crime. It is no more entitled to respect than is the flag of a pirate."

Mark Twain

"In his later writings Trevelyan continued to stress the importance of religion. In his Romanes Lecture at Oxford, he argued that religious differences were the key to understanding the history of the two parties in Britain: The Tories were fervently loyal to the Church of England, the Whigs and Liberals were more concerned to protect and promote Dissenters' rights."

David Cannadine

"Be Britain still to Britain true,
Among ourselves united;
For never but by British hands
Maun British wrangs be righted!"

Robert Burns

"Nothing in all the known world of politics is so intractable as a band of zealots, conscious that they are in a minority, yet armed by accident with the powers of a majority."

Samuel Morley

"Primarily an attitude of mind, a spiritual testament."

John Buchan on the concept of history

"The causes of the events are always more important than the events themselves."

Cicero

"The British Empire was the most benign Empire of all."

Keith Davidson

"Europe must realise that after the hard landing free trade will no longer be feasible."

Michael White

"The institutions of the USA are far more frozen into immobility than those of almost all other states in 2002…

Historians who believe in the supremacy of high politics and great individuals have a hard case in America. So, since the end of the USSR, the USA has quietly prepared to function as the world's only superpower. The problem is that its situation has no historical precedent, that its political system is geared to the ambitions and reactions of New Hampshire primaries and provincial protectionisms. Nobody controls the USA today'."

Eric Hobsbawm

"The ultimate foundation of a free society is the binding tie of cohesive sentiment. Such a sentiment is fostered by all those agencies of mind and spirit which may serve to gather up the tradition of a people, transmit them from generation to generation, and thereby create that continuity of a treasured common life which constitutes a civilisation."

Felix Frankfurter

"Politics are close to morals."

Maurice Bowra

"Democracy – 'All the ills of democracy can be cured by more democracy.'"

Alfred E. Smith

"Government of the people by the people."

Abraham Lincoln

"What is democracy? An aristocracy of blackguards."

Byron

"Democracy substitutes election by the incompetent many for appointment by the corrupt few."
George Bernard Shaw

"1958 was six years after the end of meat rationing and six years before the introduction of capital gains tax."
Charles Gordon

"Political parties, he could not have failed to notice, had a way of absorbing people, and saving them the trouble of thinking for themselves."
John Peyton on Solly Zuckerman

"The world may yet regret that, faced with Rosa Luxemburg's alternative of socialism or barbarism, it decided against socialism."
Eric Hobsbawm

"One hears from time to time much shallow talk about the elimination of politics as though politics – the free exchange of opinion regarding the best policy for life of society – were not the essence of a free and vigorous people."
Felix Frankfurter

"Never be separated from the Americans."
Winston Churchill

"Most people in the west, certainly everyone in Israel, would agree that the Palestine suicide bombers who kill women and children are terrorists. Not many people remember when Palestine, as the land of Israel was once called, was in that obscure state a British Protectorate. Were the Jewish members of the Stern Gang, those who hanged a British sergeant with piano wire or organised the bomb in the King David Hotel with murderous results (the organisation in which Prime Minister Begin started his political career), 'freedom fighters' or 'terrorists'? What, looking at the matter from an entirely neutral standpoint, would we call them now?"

John Mortimer

"I want my part today to make a gesture to the Country … and say to them: we have our majority; we believe in the justice of this Bill which has been brought in to-day, but we are going to withdraw our hand, and we are not going to push our political advantage home at a moment like this. Suspicion which has prevented stability in Europe is the one poison that is preventing stability at home, and we offer the country today this: We, at any rate, are not going to fire the first shot. We stand for peace."

Stanley Baldwin

"Suggestions that Solly (Zuckerman) was a serious left-winger and even a member of the Communist party hardly ring true; he laughed too easily and questioned too readily."

John Peyton

"We have very satisfactory political information from the whole West – and await calmly the decisive opinions of the People as expressed at the ballot boxes next month. Ours is an agitating life under institutions so thoroughly popular. But the great mass of society is very sagacious about its interests and rights and, though liable to be misled for a time, soon

acquire further light – bring judgement to the correction of feeling – and place the ship of state in the true track to ensure the greatest good for the greatest number."
Levi Woodbury

"Where there are a number of laws drawn up with great exactitude, it is proof that the city is badly administered; for the inhabitants are compelled to frame laws in great numbers as a barrier against offences."
Socrates

"The general breakdown of capitalism after that speech by Mr Ted Heath, who actually was mainly responsible for the collapse of the British economy. Heath coined the phrase 'the unacceptable face of capitalism', which had put him in power …The unacceptable face of capitalism was something which Heath knew nothing about… And then you had the petrol crisis, at which point the British Index reached 150. The day after Dunkirk it was 350! So, you can imagine the over-compensation for this sudden increase in petrol prices; the whole of Britain collapsed, from a financial point of view. The change of government happened about that time."
Sir Gordon White

"Why should the rich, especially in countries like ours where they now glory in injustice and inequality, bother about anyone except themselves? What political parasites do they need to fear if they allow welfare to erode and the protection of those who read it to atrophy? This is the chief effect of the disappearance of even a very bad socialist region from the globe."
Eric Hobsbawm

Unfortunately, in the West we are the prisoners of our own logic. This condemns us to commit avoidable errors, for it is only through our mistakes that we change our policies."

Michael White

"Class is a life sentence as inescapable as any caste system."

A Marxist historian

"Don't you remember my first and unbreakable law of democratic politics? Bad people doing good things – the best hope left for civilisation."

Andrew Marr

"Politicians do make it very hard to have deeply held political beliefs."

John Mortimer

"A revolution is like a bicycle, if it doesn't go forward it falls down."

Mao Zedong

"In a strange way this force seems at present to be blocked. Perhaps President Yeltsin has a daemon; perhaps Deng Xiaoping does. But the west seems to have no daemons. There does not seem to be a genius whispering into President Clinton's ear, or in Chancellor Kohl's. Daemonic inspiration is absent, one would suppose, from the present House of Commons. Nor are there great creative artists easy to discover in the modern world."

John Gray

"As for my studies of communism – I think I have learned a great deal about it, but I haven't written them yet. I am particularly grateful to you for your observation about the compromising attitude of the Italians compared to the theological attitude of the French."

Hugh Trevor-Roper

"Four rules of politics in the Middle East:
 1. Always keep the initiative
 2. Always exploit the inevitable
 3. Always keep 'in' with the 'outs'
 4. Never stand between a dog and the lamppost."

Stewart Browne

"My Parkinson rider is that distrust between parties increases in direct proportion to the increase in paperwork."

Charles Gordon

"The Moscow regime supported the ANC struggle, financed and armed it for decades when there was no foreseeable prospect of its success or of Soviet benefit. A devotion to colonial liberation was probably the last relic of the spirit of world revolution."

Eric Hobsbawm

"I do believe that the modern American Presidency makes sense as a political system only when it is seen to be a latter-day version of a British mediaeval monarchy, and I commend this approach to its loyal American subjects. Thus armed, they will be less bothered by the frustrations that usually attend the conventional method of measuring the incumbent against the constitutional yardstick. I am not denigrating the United States Constitution; as a foreign correspondent who has worked in too many countries, I am immensely respectful of it. Nevertheless, it is not always helpful when discussing the modern Presidency, and therefore the modern American system, and for a further understanding one must return to the mediaeval past of the British monarchy… the main difference between the modern American President and a mediaeval monarch is that there has been a steady increase rather than diminution of his power. In comparative historical terms the United States has been moving steadily backward."

Louis Heren

"'Britain,' he said, 'is a very difficult country to move, Mr Hyndman, a very difficult country indeed, and one, in which there is more disappointment to be looked for than success.'"

Henry Hyndman quoting Benjamin Disraeli

"Everywhere today in Europe and the Americas there are urbane and lusty spirits – comrades in the Country of the Mind – who feed and live on this legacy of mental freedom, aesthetic sensitivity, friendly and sympathetic understanding; forgiving life its tragedies, embracing its joys of sense, mind and soul; and hearing ever in their hearts, hymns of hate and above the canon's roar the song of the Renaissance."

Will Durant

"If you don't get a war, you don't get a great general."

Theodore Roosevelt

"Pax Britannica was based on trade protected by the Navy – 100 years of peace."
Unattributed

"To those who have never had to take such decisions, may I say to them that they are taken with a heavy heart, in the knowledge of the manifold dangers, but with tremendous pride in the professionalism and courage of our armed forces. But there is something else one feels as well. That is a sense of this country's destiny, the centuries of history and experience which ensure that when principles have to be defended, when good has to be upheld, when evil has to be overcome, then Britain will take up arms."
Margaret Thatcher

"Confusion was immediately restored."
Expression used in the Second World War

"Gratuitous information from Clore was unprecedented."
Charles Gordon on Charles Clore

"In the 21st century, survival will be more complicated and precarious than ever before, and the ethics required of us must be correspondingly sophisticated."
Oscar Arias

"Our hands may be active, but our consciences are at rest."
Winston Churchill

"No drums they wished, whose thoughts were tied
To girls and jobs and mother,
Who rose and drilled and killed and died,
Because they saw no other.
Who died without the hero's throb,
And if they trembled, hid it,
Who did not fancy much their job
But thought it best, and did it."

Michael Thwaites

"In the autumn of 1961, after Kennedy had won the election, I was invited to attend a conference of the Pugwash Movement at Stowe, Vermont. Its founders were primarily Western scientists, many of them conscience stricken about the part they had played in the invention of nuclear weapons but all quite properly terrified at the possibility of nuclear war and anxious to promote the cause of disarmament by establishing contact with their Soviet colleagues. Towards the end of the 1950s the possibility of limited measures, at least, to prevent the possibility of 'unintended' nuclear war or the proliferation of nuclear weapons, was being taken more seriously in government circles. The concept of 'disarmament', with all its unfortunate pre-war implications, was yielding to that, more respectable, of 'arms control'. The Soviet government regarded this as a God given opportunity for 'peace' propaganda. Questions about inspection and control of arms reduction were brushed aside. Nonetheless the Americans persevered. The Russians were just as frightened of us as we were of them."

Michael Howard

"Overseas, the tentacles of American economic and military power now reached every corner of the globe, as exemplified by the creation of a gargantuan network of US military installations and bases – in south America, throughout the Pacific, across the middle East, South Asia, even in Africa."

Fredrik Logevall

"Now tell us about the war
And what they fought each other for."

Robert Southey

"Why did they die? Not for the Atlantic Charter, not to make a land fit for heroes to live in. They fought ungrudgingly and, in a sense, unwillingly. They could do no other and no words could pay adequate tribute to what they did – and they did not like doing it. These heirs of disillusion fought, and died, to give us a chance.

Donald Hughes, Headmaster, Rydal School

"Looking back down the long corridor of the years, I can't remember England ever being so united as it was during the War, or so hopeful as during the Attlee Government. Politics had changed, to conform to some of our dearly held beliefs."

John Mortimer

"You must despise your enemy strategically but respect him tactically."

Mao Zedong

"We need a moral equivalent for war."

Henry James

"I saw the spires of Oxford
As I was passing by,
The grey spires of Oxford
Against a pearl grey sky;
My heart was with the Oxford men
Who went abroad to die."

Winifred Mary Letts

Evil, Anger and Despair

"I and the public know,
What all schoolchildren learn,
Those to whom evil is done
Do evil in return."

W.H. Auden

"I'm suspicious of viciousness. It often conceals a lack of content, and anger is only useful if it explains something."

Ian Hislop

"Only a bad person needs to repent; only a good person can repent perfectly. The worse you are the more you need it and the less you can do it."

C.S. Lewis

"There was never anything by the wit of man so well devised, or so sure established, which in continuance of time hath not been corrupted."

The Book of Common Prayer

"Corruption can undo everything else we are trying to do."

Dr Norman Burlaug

"It appears always easier to recognise inhumanity when it lies on someone else's doorstep."
Mahatma Gandhi

"Above all, beware of those who spend their time nosing out the alleged sins of other people, in order to punish them. They are mad, bad and dangerous to know."
Lord Boothby

"Beware the anger of a patient man."
Arthur Ashe

"We were taught at Marlborough that the sins of the fathers are wrought upon the sons even until the third and fourth generations."
Bruce Chatwin

"A man and what he loves and builds have but a day and then disappear; nature cares not – and renews the annual round untired. It is the old law, sad but not bitter. Only when man destroys the life and beauty of nature, there is the outrage."
G.M. Trevelyan

"The best revenge is not to be like them."
Arthur Quiller-Couch

"Before you embark on a journey of revenge, dig two graves."
Proverb

"But really! Is our civilization so lacking in self-confidence that it cannot allow itself to forgive and forget? This common-law malefactor who can extract from his misfortune enough strength to live and to teach others how to live inspires my respect. Far more than I feel, at any rate, for those who knife him in the back. I don't like manhunts."

François Mitterand on Paul Touvier, a French collaborator during WW2

"Nothing is harmless if it takes up space. Mental and spiritual space. You must get it out of your mind."

John Updike

"For more than a century now children have ceased to be brought up to become adults. Quite the contrary, and the result is that the adults of our era are brought up – we are brought up - to continue to be children. To get worked up over some sports event and grow jealous at the slightest thing. To live in a state of constant alarm and insatiable desire. To be fearful and angry. To be cowardly. To observe ourselves."

Unattributed

"Who going through the vale of misery, use it for a well."

Psalm 84:6 from *The Book of Common Prayer*

"Continuous action can defeat despair."

Eleanor Roosevelt

"We cannot despair of humanity since we are only human ourselves."

Albert Einstein

"Ben spoke without remorse and without catharsis. He had confessed enough to himself, all day and night, I knew. He talked in the dead tone of somebody describing a disaster he knows that nobody can understand who was not part of it, and the music kept playing below his voice. He had no use for himself. The glamorous hero had given up as one of life's contenders. Perhaps he was a little tired of his guilt. He spoke tersely. I think he wanted me to go."

John le Carré on his character Ben Arno Cavendish in *The Secret Pilgrim*

"Laugh a little, and teach your men to laugh … If you can't smile grin. If you can't grin keep out of the way till you can. It is a crime to despair. Live dangerously; take things as they come; dread naught, all will be well."

Winston Churchill

Life, Suffering and Death

"Life is a veil of tears."
Psalm 82

"One crowded hour of glorious life
Is worth an age without a name."
Thomas Mordant

"Life is a theatre of the absurd."
Jean-Paul Sartre

"A house unkept cannot be so distressing as a life unlived."
Rose Macaulay

"Life is no more than a fatal illness."
Siegmund Warburg

"The great object of life is sensation – to feel that we exist".
Byron

"The Glory of God is a human being fully alive."
Saint Irenaeus

"Bill saw in his (art) collection his own life story of accomplishment and adversity, pleasure and pain, serenity and struggle. He wanted his children to experience the thrill that I did doing my own thing; everybody has to find his or her own way in life" he said … 'I'm much more interested in having my children being my legacy than this art collection being my monument.'"

Daniel Schulman on Bill Koch

"You can't clad yourself in hoops of steel or iron armour against all the vicissitudes of life. If you did, it would be a very boring life. I think it's worthwhile to be vulnerable. It is worthwhile to be passionate. It is worthwhile to make mistakes. And it's worthwhile to feel as well as think. To be very human, and not to dehumanise yourself in some protective way."

George Carman

"Do not neglect your sick and elderly. Do not turn away from the handicapped and the dying. Do not push them to the margins of society. For if you do, you fail to understand an important truth. The sick, the elderly, the handicapped and the dying teach us that weakness is a creative part of human living, and that suffering can be embraced with no loss of dignity."

Pope Paul II

"Like all very selfish people she slipped easily into the role of martyr."

Byron

"Waiting is painful. Forgetting is painful. But not knowing which to do is the worst kind of suffering."

Paulo Coelho

"Jackson is arguably the greatest writer to have ever sat in the (American Supreme) Court but something deep and terrible haunted him. In the midst of comfort and the acclaim which attended his performances, he was the loneliest figure, but one I've met, and, with the end in sight and eagerly reaching for the release it would bring. I believe he considered himself fundamentally a hollow man. 'Tis sad, but I believe it true' Frankfurter would certainly have understood the reference to T S Eliot's 'The Hollow Men', one of the iconic modernist poems of his generation. It suggested death before death: a futility of existence that could not have been more unlike Frankfurter's own zest for life… It hinted, in short, that Jackson died believing he had been a failure."

Noah Feldman on Andrew Jackson

"One deals with one's own pain – there is no effort without it."

Teddy Roosevelt

"A retrospective shudder."

Friedrich Nietzsche, recalling a near disaster

"I'm accustomed to my deafness
To my dentures I'm resigned
I can cope with my bifocals,
But – Oh dear! – I miss my mind."

John Sparrow

"The ruthless self-absorption of old age."

Peter Green

"Old age is not for sissies."
Janet Adam Smith

"There seems to be no limit at all to their endurance."
Ali Az-Naimi

"Suffering is infinitely more powerful than the law of the jungle for converting the opponent and opening his ears which are otherwise shut to the voice of reason … To our most bitter opponents we say we shall match your capacity to inflict suffering by our capacity to endure suffering. We shall meet your physical force with soul force. Do to us what you will, and we shall continue to love you … but be assured that we will wear you down by our capacity to suffer."
Mahatma Gandhi

"The past falters and dies by little steps. Then it has gone, and old men go home disappointed."
James Rebanks

"My sword I give to him that shall succeed me in my pilgrimage."
John Bunyan

"He was a man, take him for all in all, I shall not look upon his like again."
Hamlet

"Sheep without a shepherd;
When the snow shuts out the sky –
Oh, why did you leave us, Owen?
Why did you die?"

An Irish ballad

LIFE, SUFFERING AND DEATH

"The long days store up many things nearer to grief than joy
… Death at the last the deliverer.
Next best by far when one has seen the light
Is to go thither swiftly whence he came."

Sophocles

"Brief as life is, there never yet was or will be a man who does not wish more than once to die rather than to live."

Herodoctus

"We must do today what we cannot do so well tomorrow."

William Stanley Jevons

"The ancient Romans believed that the manner of a man's death is as important as the manner of his life, and I'd like to have a kind of heroic death."

John Aspinall

"Walking in a garden
At the break of day
Mary asked the gardener
where the body lay
but he turned toward her
smiled at her and said:
'Mary, spring is here to stay
Only death is dead."

Hilary Greenwood

"Too many things go wrong."

Tony Hancock

"Death be not proud."
John Donne

"It's not that I'm afraid to die: I just don't want to be there when it happens."
Woody Allen

"But this denial of death bothers me. I feel that a society which hides death from the eyes of the living, paints it over like a lie, removes it from daily awareness is not magnifying life but corrupting it. Birth and death are the two wings of time. How can a man's spiritual search come to fulfilment if he ignores these dimensions?"
François Mitterand

"Yet each man kills the thing he loves."
Oscar Wilde

"The basic fear remains. It lurks at the back of every Christian head. The fear of being forgotten by God, uncared for by God. The fear that God's control ends at death's gate. The fear that for all the brave words, there is extinction … Beneath the serenity of the face of Christ as he accepts the welcome and the proclamation of his kingship, there is an acceptance of another kind; acceptance of human apprehension as the dark clouds gather round him, the loneliness which the approach of death brings with it to the solitary soul, for dying is not a group activity and nobody can shoulder the burden for you; its quiet inevitability, its certainty, its deliberate speed and its effectiveness …

And he goes on to say something else, about you and me. For true life in him there has to be true death, the solitary grain of what has to fall into the ground and die, it has to experience that solitary experience so as to be solitary no more. There has to be the last surrender, there has to be a falling, we must allow ourselves to be dropped from the hand of a faithful and loving Creator into the good earth of his caring, knowing that all things are in his hands, grave and resting place alike. When we allow it, he can act mightily. For herein lies his promise, that remarkable promise Christ makes precisely at this point: 'Where I am, there will my servant be'."

Reverend John Andrew

"A man's works should be remembered and his life forgotten."

F.E. Smith on death

"Everybody wants to go to heaven, but nobody wants to die."

Arthur Ashe

"The worst thing about the approach of death isn't death itself and what it may or may not bring, it's the fact that one can no longer fantasise about things still to come."

Javier Marías Franco

"To live in the hearts of those we leave behind is not to die."

On a bench in the churchyard of St Paul's, Covent Garden

"God is good. Nothing more can be done. Death is not the end of it all but the beginning."

Cardinal Cushing

"As you age a degree of depression is inevitable as you gradually approach death."

Unattributed

"I have often observed that the merriest faces are to be seen in mourning coaches."

Jonathan Swift

"Do not go gentle into that good night. Rage, rage against the dying of the light!"

Dylan Thomas

"So, what happens when you die? 'Simply, you become dust. Dust. And I am actually looking forward to it.' Why? 'Life is still hard, fatiguing, and things go wrong. A little bit here, a little bit there.'"

V.S. Naipaul

"Grow old along with me!
The best is yet to be,
The last of life, for which the first was made:
Our times are in His hand
Who saith: 'A whole I planned,
Youth shows but half; trust God: see all, nor be afraid!"

Robert Browning

"If I must die,
I will encounter darkness like a bride
And Bring it in my arms."

William Shakespeare

"Aboriginals, when they feel death close, will make a kind of pilgrimage (sometimes a distance of thousands of miles) back to their 'conception site; their 'centre', the place where they belong."

Bruce Chatwin

"Nothing resembles a person as much as the way he dies."

Gabriel Garcia Marquez

"It is foolish to waste lamentations upon the closing phase of human life. Noble spirits yield themselves willingly to the successively falling shades which carry them to a better world or to oblivion."

Winston Churchill

"Do not grieve for me too much. I am a spirit confident of my rights. Death is only an incident, and not the most important which happens to us in this state of being. On the whole, especially since I met you my darling one, I have been happy, and you have taught me how noble a woman's heart can be. If there is anywhere else, I shall be on the lookout for you. Meanwhile look forward, feel free, rejoice in life, cherish the children, guard my memory. God bless you – Goodbye. W."

Winston Churchill, note left for his wife in the event of his death in the First World War

"In life, only death and taxes are inevitable."

Benjamin Franklin

"The recently dead … have a brief life as ghosts, then the grave closes over them. Few return."

Noel Annan

"I want death to find me planting my cabbages – caring little for it and even less about the imperfections of my garden."
Michel de Montaigne

"When the legends die, the dreams end. When the dreams end, there is no more greatness."
Hal Borland

"Desire and meaning were the pillars of life; and once they failed him there would be no further purpose in living."
A.L. Rowse

"The destruction of the soul is vanity – the destruction of the mind is poverty."
Bob Marley

"I thought how he was facing death with stoicism, with detachment and with faith. His faith assured him that he would pass into another existence. The Master's vanities had been burned away (cancer), he was detached, unselfish as he came towards his death, and yet the desire to be remembered was intact."
C.P. Snow on John William Mackail, Master of Balliol College, Oxford

"He had done his best and taken his rest. And that, my friends, is all that is required of any of us."
John McCain

"The stars know the time when we die."
Bruce Chatwin

"If I laugh at any mortal being, Tis that I may not weep."
Byron

"She had only meant to pin a notice up in the porch, but had found herself coming in. It was a moment of stillness, that was all. Just a way to step outside your life for a few minutes. Who was it who talked about places where prayer had been valid? This was surely one of them. Hundreds of years of prayer had filled the space around her, bounded by the building's cool walls and tall windows: hundreds of years of village breath, Lodeshill's (the village) faithful surrounded her, all loved in their time and their passing mourned; remembered for a few lifetimes, then lost. A name scratched into the back of a pew. A stone slab from which the legend had been worn away by centuries of feet."
Melissa Harrison

"Does the road wind up-hill all the way?
Yes to the very end.
Will the day's journey take the whole long day?
From morn to night, my friend."
Christina Georgina Rossetti

"When you look back, and forgetfully wonder
What you were like in your work and your play."
Edward Ernest Bowen

"Full lasting is the song, though he,
The singer, passes lasting too,
For souls not lent in usury
The Rapture of the formal view."
George Meredith

"On the idle hill of summer,
Sleepy with the flow of streams,
Far I hear the steady drummer,
Drumming like a noise in dreams …"

A.E. Housman

"Work while it is yet day, for the night cometh in which no man can work."

A L Rowse

"Each man's death diminishes me,
For I am involved in mankind
Therefore send not to know
For whom the bell tolls,
It tolls for thee."

John Donne

"When you are old and grey, and full of sleep,
And dodging by the fire, take down this book
And slowly read, and dream of the soft look
Your eyes once had, and of their shadows deep."

W.B. Yeats

"Death had to take him sleeping otherwise a fight."

About Teddy Roosevelt

"He loved his youth, and his youth has become eternal. Debonair and brilliant and brave, he is now part of that immortal England which knows not age or weariness or defeat."

John Buchan on Raymond Asquith, who died in WW1

LIFE, SUFFERING AND DEATH

"Churchill told Jock Colville in 1953 that he would die on the anniversary of his father's death, and he did."

Andrew Roberts

"Beyond the Wheat and Harvest
of fruit upon the bough,
I recognize old Autumn
riding on a plough.
The year has passed its zenith
and now it must decline;
Earth's had her share of summer
As I have had of mine."

M.M. Kaye

"The woods are lovely, dark and deep
But I have promises to keep,
And miles to go before I sleep,
And miles to go before I sleep."

Robert Frost

"Clay lies still, but blood's a rover
Breath's aware that will not keep,
Up, lad, when the journey's over,
There'll be time enough to sleep."

A.E. Housman

Character, Experience and Words of Wisdom

"You may be whatever you resolve to be."
Stonewall Jackson

"Failure and Success are, in their different ways, equal tasks of a man's character. My Right Honourable Friend has overcome both triumphantly. These twists and changes of political fortune were not mere accidents. They were the very fabric of his life. Like the prophets of old, he saw into the future with uncanny prescience both before, during and after the War. So, we honour the whole Man – what he has done, what he has tried to do and what he is. If I were to try to sum up his true character, I can think of no words more appropriate than those which he has himself written on the flyleaf of each volume of his History of the Second World War. 'In War: Resolution. In Defeat: Defiance. In Victory: Magnanimity. In Peace: Goodwill.' The author called those words 'Morals of the Work'. In fact, Sir, they are the story of his life."

Harold Macmillan on Winston Churchill

"I have known finer and greater characters, wiser philosophers, more understanding personalities, but no greater man."
President Dwight D. Eisenhower on Winston Churchill

"He was a child of nature. He venerated tradition, but ridiculed convention."

General Lord Ismay on Winston Churchill

"Beliefs about how you live your life, matters of private decision, views best kept for private enjoyment, prejudice or entertainment, can't be imposed by the operation of the criminal law. Over himself, over his own body and mind, the individual is sovereign."

John Stuart Mill

"One of the finest minds in Britain until he makes it up."

David Owen on Enoch Powell

"If you know nothing about people, you can believe anything about them."

Dervla Murphy

"The thought of him has always slightly irritated me. Of course he was a wonderfully all-round man, but the act of walking round him has always tired me."

Max Beerbohm on William Morris

"His heroism lay in his ceaseless attempts to heal differences, to prevent atrocities so far as he could, to keep his temper and to retain his belief in the justice of the cause."

John Mortimer on Byron

"A man's character is like a credit balance at the bank from which he can draw from time to time."

Lord Birkett

"When Socrates spoke, the people said how inspiring, but when Demosthenes spoke, the people said let us march."
Adlai Stevenson

"People are frail."
Arthur Ashe

"I suspect that we all (all politicians at least) have in us something of the 'having one's cake and eating it' spirit which is reputed to have afflicted the well-known Labour peer who wrote a book on Humility, walked down Piccadilly without seeing it in Hatchard's bookshop, went in, sent for the manager and demanded to know why it was not in the windows."
Roy Jenkins

"True wisdom does not always … consist in universal sympathy and tolerance. The world is moved in the first instance by those who see one side of a question only – although the services of those who see both are indispensable for effecting a settlement."
G.M. Trevelyan

"'Great people have an inbuilt instinct about how long they're going to live – a sort of rhythm to the way they rule their life.' This explained the disciplined economy of his writing, his manic behaviour, his impatient appetite for experience. 'He was like a little firework all the time.'"
Pam Bell on Bruce Chatwin

"When the fight begins within himself
A man's worth something."

A.L. Rowse

"For it was Logan who afterwards re-interested me, in a time when the war had separated me from desperate academic study, in style and the world of sensation, and enabled me thus to fill in the hard structural pattern of thought I had thus evolved; and how can I express adequate gratitude for such an experience? Who showed me that life is short, and three parts routine, and most of it comedy, and can only be saved from triviality and given significance by some ideal to which all else or at least much else including humane pleasures and meritorious claims, and especially power and success must be sacrificed, as by the merchant who sold out to reinvest all in one pearl of great price; and that style is an ideal of this sacrifice."

Hugh Trevor-Roper on Logan Pearsall Smith

"I am convinced that the only thing a man of fifty knows that a man of twenty does not, both of them being equally endowed, has nothing to do with an accumulation of knowledge: It has to do with guessing a little more certainly how human beings are likely to act."

Alistair Cooke

"But I still think that a personality is tested by being tested. You understand your personality when you pass through tests of one sort or another."

Nicholas Henderson

"But it is the same with man as with the tree. The more he seeks to rise into the height and light, the more vigorously do his roots struggle earthward, downward, into the dark, the deep – into evil."

Friedrich Nietzsche

"My father had a great rule of thumb: bet on what you think a man will do rather than what he says he will do, and you will be right more often than not."

Edward Kennedy

"The sheer weight of one person's personality begins, sooner or later, to make everyone pause to consider if what is proposed to be done will meet with that person's approval."

Victor Peers on Sidney Bernstein

"He was another of those whose liking for me made me think better of myself."

Freddie Ayer on George Orwell

"American banks are very aggressive, they're of course always looking for what they call the three C's: Character, Capability and Credibility. Character is the most important thing you have to establish, because they want to know that if everything goes wrong, you're going to maintain your endeavours to pay back the money they've lent you."

Gordon White

"I would never want to belong to any club that would have someone like me for a member."

Groucho Marx

"He thought enthusiasm even more important than originality."
Noel Annan on J.J. Thomson

"Noel could not escape being public spirited."
Nicolas Henderson on Noel Annan

"Most of the triumphs of a man in adverse circumstances are triumphs of character rather than intelligence."
Siegmund Warburg

"He always trusted experience as the greatest creator of character."
Eunice Shriver on Joe Kennedy

"The first thing is character before money or anything else because a man I do not trust could not get money from me on all the bonds in Christendom."
John Pierpoint Morgan

"I think the main thing was that when he (Jack Kennedy) talked to you, he looked you straight in the eye and his attention never wandered. He was interested in finding out what I was doing there – why was I there. It was a drawing-me-outing, it was undivided attention."
Anita Marcus

"I noted the Cornish trait of naivete in the egoism – the simplicity of the assumption that everyone would be as interested in his doings as himself; we all have the same guileless trait. More sophisticated types are not so keen."
A.L. Rowse

"He knows what he wants, but he also wants to hear what others have to say."

Henry Angest on Andrew Salmon

"Yet I doubt not thro' the ages one increasing purpose runs, And the thoughts of men are widen'd with the process of the suns."

Tennyson

"The childhood shows the man, as morning shows the day."

John Milton

"In years to come you will wish you had asked these questions; ignorance is a curse lying in wait for the younger generation, for those who forgot to ask."

Hannah Rothschild

"If only the young knew and the old were able."

Oscar Wilde

"Encouragement is the most important gift one individual can give to another, particularly when it is handed from the old to the young."

Tony Benn

"No system of ethics holds water: they all spring leaks when tested. But when he (Bernard Williams) asked himself which of these systems come nearest to giving us criteria for leading a moral life, he discarded the utilitarian ethics elaborated by Richard Hare or the contractual ethics of John Rawls. Nor did the moral imperative in Kant's reason seem any better."

Noel Annan

"We must allow the child to take the reins of our lives. The child knows that each day is different from every other day. We have to allow it to feel loved again. We must please this child – even if this means that we act in ways we are not used to, in ways that may seem foolish to others. Remember that human wisdom is madness in the eyes of God. But if we listen to the child who lives in our soul, our eyes will grow bright. If we do not lose contact with that child, we will not lose contact with life."

Paul Coelho

"Nothing ever becomes real until it is experienced."

John Keats

"Experience is the name everyone gives to their mistakes."

Oscar Wilde

"The wider our experience, the deeper our tolerance."

Taken from a calendar

"Wisdom and Backbone are factors independent of culture."

Joseph Conrad

"You're lucky in life if you pick the right heroes."

Warren Buffett

"To understand the world is a basic human longing, powerful and urgent. The idea that there is rarely any point to anything is not to be borne. So, the child in this story looked back and tried to understand. Here is some of what was understood; that you sometimes have to leave it behind and enter the poetic world where making sense is optional; that things are often not what they seem; that language is precarious, that sometimes there is not a name for what you feel; that you take love where you find it; that even when everything is concealed you can end up being open to the world."

Jennie Erdal

"Reason cannot prevail where reason cannot penetrate."

Peter Quennell

"Memory and Desire are the twin pillars of existence."

A.L. Rowse

"Realism, like reality is infinite (that is, there are as many versions of it as there are people in the world) and by the same token attention to external appearances differs according to who is doing the attending"

Phillip Lopate

"A word is worth one coin; silence is worth two."

The Talmud

"Her wrinkles are the credentials of her humanity."

George Bernard Shaw on Eleonora Duse

"Teddy, let me give you some advice. Follow it, and you'll be much happier for the rest of your life. Never listen to a phone call that isn't meant for you. Never read a letter that isn't meant for you. Never pay attention to a comment that isn't meant for you. Never violate people's privacy – You will save

yourself a great deal of anguish. You might not understand this now, but you will later on."
Joseph Kennedy

"The good are so hard to the clever, the clever so rude to the good."
Miss Wordsworth by Albert Herring

"So, there's no better occupation than listening, only interrupting and asking for further and better particulars."
John Mortimer

"Equality exists in the treatment of unequal things unequally."
Aristotle

"Man is spirit."
Winston Churchill

"I have a simple philosophy. Fill what's empty, empty what's full, and scratch where it itches."
Alice Roosevelt Longworth

"No mind is thoroughly well organised that is deficient in a sense of humour."
Samuel Taylor Coleridge

"A man's assumptions are more important than his pronouncements."
Percy Heywood

"When people are least sure, they are often most dogmatic."
J.K. Galbraith

"The world is a comedy to those that think, a tragedy to those who feel."

Horace Walpole

"Pain that cannot forget
Falls drop by drop
upon the heart
until in our despair
there comes wisdom
through the awful
grace of God."

Aeschylus

"The child is father of the man."

William Wordsworth

"Everybody is important, but nobody is very important."

Kurt Vonnegut

"Flattery is alright if you don't inhale."

Adlai Stevenson

"The Life of the law has not been logic; it has been experience."

Oliver Wendell Holmes

"Men had to discover their identity before they could express themselves."

Noel Annan

"To be what we are, and become what we are capable of becoming is the only end in life."

Robert Louis Stevenson

"The world is divided into people who do things and people who get the credit. Try if you can, to belong to the first class: there is far less competition."

Siegmund Warburg

"A man does not show his greatness by being at one extremity, but rather by touching both at once."

Blaise Pascal

"Genius is the infinite capacity for taking pains."

Thomas Carlyle

"Progress in thought is progress towards simplicity."

Paraphrase of Thor Heyerdahl

"One sign of mental maturity is to comprehend the power and delight of simplicity."

Vernon Howard

"Any intelligent fool can invent further complications, but it takes a genius to attain, or recapture, simplicity."

E.F. Schumacher

"The world is a lunatic asylum for the Universe."

Voltaire

"To the young – beware of imagination. To be led by it is to follow a rainbow. Beware of indecision, it neutralises every virtue."

Lady Anne Barnard

"Culture is what you have left when you have forgotten everything."

M. Herriot

"The chains of habit are too weak to be felt until they are too strong to be broken."

Dr Johnson

"Life would be dull without human error."

Evelyn Waugh

"If you have nothing good to say about anyone, come and sit with me."

Alice Roosevelt Longworth

"The World will not get better on its own."

A.E. Housman

"Whatever you are, be that,
Whatever you say, be true,
Straightforward act,
Be honest, in fact,
Be nobody else but you."

Gilbert and Sullivan.

Printed in Great Britain
by Amazon

92dd1f27-a760-4f25-8d0d-4f5ca5917345R01